Commitment to Sustainability

OPEN

BOOK

Ooligan Press is committed to becoming an academic leader in sustainable publishing practices. Using both the classroom and the business, we will investigate, promote, and utilize sustainable products, technologies, and practices as they relate to the production and distribution of our books. We hope to lead and encourage the publishing community by our example. Making sustainable choices is not only vital to the future of our industry — it's vital to the future of our world.

OpenBook Series

One component of our sustainability campaign is the OpenBook Series. *Untangling the Knot: Queer Voices on Marriage, Relationships & Identity* is the seventh book in the series, so named to highlight our commitment to transparency on our road toward sustainable publishing. We believe that disclosing the impacts of the choices we make will not only help us avoid unintentional greenwashing, but also serve to educate those who are unfamiliar with the choices available to printers and publishers.

Efforts to produce this series as sustainably as possible focus on paper and ink sources, design strategies, efficient and safe manufacturing methods, innovative printing technologies, supporting local and regional companies, and corporate responsibility of our contractors.

All titles in the OpenBook Series will have the OpenBook logo on the front cover and a corresponding OpenBook Environmental Audit inside, which includes a calculated paper impact from the Environmental Paper Network.

D1472062

OpenBook Environmental Audit
Untangling the Knot: Queer Voices on Marriage, Relationships & Identity
Figures are calculated for a print run of 2,000 paperbacks.

	Chemicals	Greenhouse Gases	Energy	Fiber	Waste
Paper[†]					
Cover Paper: 10pt Kallima C1S. 112 lbs. used.	Under 1-lb. of volatile organic compounds and under 1-lb. or hazardous air pollutants produced in paper production.	314 lbs. carbon dioxide equivalent used in production.[‡] Tembec is committed to being carbon-neutral by 2015.	2 million BTUs used in production;[‡] Manufactured by Tembec in Canada.	Paper produced from approximately one tree.[†]	108 lbs. of solid waste produced in paper production.[‡]
Text paper: 55# FRP Heritage Tradebook Natural; 30% PCW. 1,969 lbs used.	1-lb. reduction of volatile organic compounds; 1-lb. reduction of hazardous air pollutants.[‡]	611-lb. reduction of carbon dioxide equivalent.[‡]	3 million BTU reduction in net energy.[‡] Manufactured by Flambeau River Papers in Wisconsin.	1-ton reduction in virgin fiber use, the equivalent of about 7 trees.[‡]	222-lb. reduction in solid waste; 3,313-gallon reduction in water consumption.[‡]
Printing & Binding					
23" and 34.5" sheets printed on Timsons T32 press by United Graphics, Inc. in Mattoon, Illinois.	Hot glues in perfect binding contain paraffin waxes, petroleum, clay, and titanium dioxide.	UGI uses Barsol solvents to clean their presses.	Timsons Quick Make Ready system reduces downtime, and make-ready and bindery waste.		
Perfect bound with Henkel adhesives. 4 lbs. used.					Lamination reduces damage to books, which reduces the number of unread, returned copies.
Cover finished with matte lamination film manufactured by Transilwrap Company, Inc. 1,781 ft. used.					Transilwrap Company, Inc. uses recycling programs to reduce factory waste.
Ink					
Vision Series offset printing ink manufactured by Alden & Ott Printing Inks in the United States. 19 lbs. used.	Vision Series ink are vegetable-based.				

This Open Book Audit—performed by Ooligan Press—stems from our commitment to transparency in our efforts to produce a line of books using the most sustainable materials and processes available to us.

All quantities and material specifications supplied by United Graphics, Inc.

[†] Environmental impact estimates made using the EPN Paper Calculator tool at http://www.papercalculator.org.

[‡] Compared to paper made with 100% virgin fiber.

Praise for *Untangling the Knot*

"The essays in this collection show why we all deserve the right to marry and why some of us will not wish to do so. The mélange of viewpoints demonstrates the complexity of the defining struggle of gay rights in our time, showing that it is not the monolith that political expedience often makes it seem. These writers speak with passion about love, law, loss, generational differences, and identity. This is an urgent and timely book."
—Andrew Solomon, author of *Far from the Tree: Parents, Children and the Search for Identity* and *The Noonday Demon: An Atlas of Depression*

"*Untangling the Knot* is a valuable contribution not only to discussions of same-sex marriage but also to debates about priorities for the LGBTQ movement and indeed for all movements for social change. The essays here—many by trans* and queer folk living in unconventional and creative family and community structures—are not theoretical but rather honest and moving stories of people's lives, dilemmas, and solutions. The collection is a joy to read and fruitful to contemplate."
—Amy Hoffman, author of *Lies About My Family* and editor in chief of *Women's Review of Books*

"Moving and heartfelt, *Untangling the Knot* is a validating reality check for every queer activist who has been pushed to the margins for challenging the tidy and normalized sound bites about marriage. Talented storytellers with remarkably diverse identities and perspectives are reclaiming the pressing issues that have been masked by mainstream marriage fever."
—Abigail Garner, author of *Families Like Mine: Children of Gay Parents Tell It Like It Is*

"There is no denying the debate surrounding marriage equality and what it means for LGBTQ families is complex and layered with varying interpretations. *Untangling the Knot* shares with readers diverse voices and views of how marriage both helps and hinders the LGBTQ civil rights movement."
—Ryan K. Sallans author of *Second Son: Transitioning Toward My Destiny, Life and Love*

Untangling the Knot is a welcome respite from the false promises of the gay marriage movement. Bracing and embracing, the essays in this collection illuminate personal, familial and structural challenges to the "we're just like you" mentality of mainstream gay politics. This book encourages us to hold onto a queer ethic that prioritizes the needs of those most vulnerable instead of settling for a place at the table of normalcy.
—Mattilda Bernstein Sycamore, author of *The End of San Francisco*

Untangling the Knot

Untangling the Knot

Queer Voices on Marriage, Relationships & Identity

EDITED BY

Carter Sickels

Ooligan
PRESS

Ooligan Press
Portland State University
Post Office Box 751, Portland, Oregon 97207
503.725.9748
ooligan@ooliganpress.pdx.edu
www.ooliganpress.pdx.edu

Library of Congress Cataloging-in-Publication Data
Untangling the knot : queer voices on marriage, relationships & identity / edited by Carter Sickels.
pages cm
ISBN 978-1-932010-75-6
1. Sexual minorities. 2. Same-sex marriage. 3. Gender identity. 4. Interpersonal relations. I. Sickels, Carter, editor.
HQ73.U58 2015
306.76--dc23
2014042978

Cover design by Stephanie Podmore
Interior design by Erika Schnatz

Printed in the United States of America
Publisher certification awarded by Green Press Initiative.
www.greenpressinitiative.org.

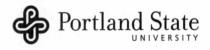

Contents

Carter Sickels

Introduction

I'm writing this the day after Oregon has legalized gay marriage, and I can't stop looking at the pictures of people lined up at the courthouse or listening to the interviews of couples who've been waiting for this moment for ten, twenty, thirty years. Today, Portland is a city of celebration. Friends who grew up in Oregon or who have lived here longer than me remember all too well the campaign of hate in 2004, when voters amended the state constitution to ban gay marriage. Today their joy for this hard-won fight ripples across the city. This summer, I'll be attending my first gay wedding, at least the first one that is legally recognized by the state.

Twenty years ago, who would have thought that queer couples would actually be able to legally tie the knot? It's been a thrilling past three years—DOMA overturned, and nineteen states and counting have granted the freedom to marry to LGBTQ couples.

My own feelings about marriage are, like so many in the LGBTQ community, complicated. I've been a part of the queer community for most of my adult life, and I never gave marriage much thought. A white transgender male, I'm privileged in ways that so many other queers are not, and yet still I must fight for recognition in both the straight and gay worlds. Over the years, instead of marriage, I've had other things on my mind: coming out to myself as trans; coming out to my family as trans and gay; accessing health care and paying for surgery; navigating whether to disclose my trans identity in a variety of situations (some of which are potentially dangerous); finding acceptance in the LGBTQ community which often disregards (or excludes) the T; and being recognized and accepted as a gay man, among other issues.

My roots are queer and feminist, and I understand the critique of marriage as a problematic, patriarchal institution. But I also understand the desire to marry, and one day perhaps my partner and I will. There are the basic legal protections marriage affords, taxes and health care and partnership and visibility—so many of us either lived through or have read the stories from the '80s about men who were denied hospital visits with their lovers dying of AIDS, who were not allowed to attend their funerals. But the freedom to marry goes beyond the legalities: why not celebrate our love with our friends and family as witnesses? Why not throw a big party? I believe queers can still *queer* marriage, turn it into something new, glittering with possibility.

Now is an exciting and interesting time to be queer in America. Marriage equality is all over the news, and acceptance of LGBTQ people is on the rise. Queers are more in the public eye. The first out gay NFL player kissed his partner on national TV— and network news channels aired it without batting an eye. Trans activists Laverne Cox and Janet Mock appear on national TV programs, openly discussing their experiences as trans women of color. Pictures of queer couples gloss the pages of major newspapers.

Yet while we in the United States are experiencing a growing acceptance of sorts, in contrast to countries that are blatantly persecuting their LGBTQ citizens—Russia and Uganda, for example—we have not achieved full-lived equality. Just read the online comments that follow any LGBTQ news story, and you'll be depressed and revolted by all the hate. Or look at the pro-discrimination efforts creeping up in places like Arizona and Oregon as well as the attempts to repeal existing antidiscrimination measures, such as in Pocatello, Idaho.

There is still so much work to be done.

Our fight for equality must be multi-issue and intersectional, and we must stand up for the most vulnerable in our community. Issues faced by the LGBTQ community include fear of living openly, lack of job protection, lack of access to equal health care, racial inequality, and poverty. LGBTQ people are far more likely than any other minority group in the United States to be victimized by violent hate crimes—this is especially true for trans women of color. Gay, lesbian, queer, and bi youth are four times more likely to attempt suicide than their straight peers; nearly *half* of young transgender people have seriously thought about taking their lives, and one-quarter report having made a suicide attempt, according to the Trevor Project. In a report published by the Human Rights Campaign, 92 percent of youth say they hear negative messages about being LGBTQ through school, the internet, and peers. Multiracial transgender and gender nonconforming people often live in extreme poverty, with 23 percent reporting a household income of less than $10,000 per year, which is almost six times the poverty rate of the general US population at 4 percent (The Task Force). There are still no federal laws protecting LGBTQ individuals from employment discrimination. Twenty-nine states still don't have laws prohibiting discrimination based on sexual orientation, and thirty-two states don't have laws prohibiting discrimination based on gender identity.

There is still so much work to be done.

Neither I nor the editors at Ooligan Press had any idea who the authors or what the content would be for this book. Ooligan's staff, made up of graduate students at Portland State University, intended *Untangling the Knot* to explore LGBTQ issues that the national marriage conversation left out, and to feature only writers from the Pacific Northwest. I joined the team as the editor, and a few months into the process, we decided to expand rather than to limit the call, and dropped the Pacific Northwest requirement.

The call for submissions was intentionally broad, to "add fresh voices to an ongoing conversation about the barriers to true queer equality. These include, but are not limited to, experiences with health care and employment, definitions of family and partnerships that extend beyond the nuclear or monogamous traditions, definitions of home, explorations of visibility, of equality, and more." With marriage in the spotlight, what issues get pushed to the back burner? Who falls through the cracks? We didn't want the book to be a platform for a debate on marriage, but rather to be a rich, open space for a multitude of voices on marriage and beyond. We wanted to know what queer people had on their minds.

Over a period of several months, as I read through the submissions, I began to see trends and themes, and slowly, a book began to take shape. I was struck by how many of the writers at least touched on the pain they've experienced in regards to their biological families; despite cultural and social shifts in acceptance of LGBTQ people, parental silence, denial, and rejection are still real and significant causes of pain for so many. Even as we create new families and find acceptance in so many aspects of our lives, we still carry with us our parents' shame. Many of the writers also remind us that despite the legalization of marriage, homophobia is still deeply entrenched in our culture. There are many queer couples who are legally married and yet are afraid to walk down the streets holding hands.

There is still so much work to be done.

Untangling the Knot examines and celebrates the complexities of queer lives. Most of these essays are personal essays about lived experiences. These twenty-six writers reflect on marriage and relationships and identities. They explore the complexities of what it means to be queer and to be married. They write about trans identities. Queer children who are bullied. Health care and battling cancer. Surviving parental or spousal abuse. They write about lack of resources and legal protections. They give testament to our LGBTQ history and ancestors, and to the power of activism. They explore the beautiful varieties of queer relationships and families. Many of the authors are married, while others hope to be, and still others have created relationships that challenge traditional definitions of marriage. What the writers in this book have in common is their desire for recognition of all aspects of their lives, and to tell the complex stories of their lived experiences.

I wanted to publish new voices and include a diversity of perspectives. The majority of the essays were unsolicited, and for at least a quarter of our writers, this is their first published work. I'm also proud to include many writers who live in rural, conservative areas of the United States—important voices the national LGBTQ conversations often leave out. And yet, there are too many gaps, too many voices and perspectives that are not in these pages—for example, the voices of people of color are underrepresented here, and I also wish we had more heard from more trans women, not only for the sake of diversity, but in order to examine the experiences of people from our communities that shed light on the issues that we should be focusing on and giving energy to.

Still, I see this book as one small step in the conversations we must have, an invitation to others to tell their stories and write about the struggles, celebrations, and issues we will continue to face long after marriage is legalized in all fifty states.

Perhaps this book is not about untangling the knot but, instead, about tangling it. And that's a good thing: queerness is about contradictions, possibilities, and challenging the old and new. Now, it's time to celebrate in Oregon, and also to continue the hard work. As US district judge Michael McShane wrote in his opinion striking down the marriage equality ban in Oregon, "Let us look less to the sky to see what might fall; rather, let us look to each other...and rise."

—*Carter Sickels May 20, 2014*

Untangling the Knot

Queer Voices on Marriage,
Relationships & Identity

Ben Anderson-Nathe

We Are Not "Just Like Everyone Else"
How the Gay Marriage Movement Fails Queer Families

I recently attended an annual fundraiser for a high-profile LGBT nonprofit organization. Since they run multiple programs, some of which I support, I had no idea until I arrived that the entire event was dedicated to raising funds for what was billed as "marriage equality" (a term I loathe for many reasons). An hour into the event, sitting at a round table full of well-intentioned, middle-aged, upper-income, white gay men, I'd had my fill of the marriage movement's rhetoric, which positioned queer people's claim to equality in the context of sameness. Based almost solely on the assertion that our relationships are no different from straight people's, the movement contends that we therefore deserve what others have. "Our love is just like your love," "Our family is just like your family," "We're committed and monogamous, just like you." These and other refrains echoed throughout the room, resulting in applause and bidding paddles being raised to donate money toward the final frontier of gay equality: marriage. Contemporary arguments for legalizing same-sex marriage are predicated on a narrative that says our relationships are just like yours. Therefore, to recognize yours but not ours is discriminatory and perpetuates inequality. And here is my struggle with that rhetoric: I am one of those well-intentioned, middle-aged, upper-income, white men, but my queer family is most certainly *not* "just like any other."

I do not want equality, with its demand that those of us on the margins must assimilate to norms that remain unquestioned, rather than transforming those norms altogether. I do not want to achieve social recognition for my family if that recognition hinges on my willingness to restructure my relationships according to the narratives and norms presented to me through conventional legal marriage. I do not support the further fracturing of queer communities such that only two-person monogamous relationships are granted validation (because *those* relationships are familiar enough to a dominant norm that the oddity of their same-sex-ness can be excused). I certainly do not want the pressing concerns of the most vulnerable members of my community (employment, housing, access to physical and mental health care, immigration protections, and so much more) to be sidelined in pursuit of the much more luxurious interests of people like me. Equity? I'm on board. But equality, and specifically equality signaled by access to marriage? Not so fast.

Much as I sometimes resist admitting it, I am an academic. I have been an activist (I hope in some ways I still am through my writing and my teaching). I am also just another queer person living with my queer family in the Pacific Northwest. From all three vantage points, I am concerned about the agenda my community seems bent on pursuing. This essay presents my attempt to tell my story, pulling all three parts of myself into alignment and adding my voice to a chorus of others in resistance to the mainstream gay rights movement's focus on "marriage equality."

Let me be clear at the outset: I am not against marriage per se. I understand and agree with many critiques of the institution itself—for its historic (and often contemporary) misogyny, its role in the service of neoliberal social and economic interests like the privatization of human caring, or its utility in legislating and policing sexuality and sexual behavior. But my primary interest here is not to dismantle the institution of marriage. Instead, I use my experiences with and in queer families to present a picture of resistance to the desperate desire of the mainstream lesbian and gay rights movement[i] to adopt a same-sex version of conventional straight marriage for the sake of social recognition, to assimilate to the hegemonic norms that structure these marriages, and to have the audacity to hold this up as the marker of equality for our communities.

The pursuit of two-person, monogamous, economically independent relationships works for many people, both within and outside queer communities. But marriage has never been the gold standard of our queer relationships; we have developed creative and adaptive structures for our relationships and families—partly out of necessity and partly out of the freedom that comes from being outside the parameters of that which is "normal." What is really at stake in the marriage debate is a larger principle: queering relationship and family. By arguing that our relationships deserve the same recognition as everyone else's only because or when we are "just like everyone else," we declare that marriage is the norm for queer relationships and the basis of "normal" queer families.

This is a position I simply cannot support. As an activist, it runs contrary to all my values related to social justice and pluralism;

the melting pot analogy, in which difference fades in favor of a single shared identity, is simply unacceptable. As a scholar, I reject claims to a single account of the human experience, a "normal" around which all Others orbit. As a queer person myself, I have lived and continue to live in families that are actually jeopardized by normalizing gay relationships and queer families only insofar as they align with a default heterosexual "everyone else."

My family and the families in my queer community are not like everyone else's. My friends' families consist of ex-lovers supporting one another long after their relationships have ended, in some cases claiming bonds of family and community with each other's new lovers (and new exes); sexually intimate relationships with more than two partners; gay men and lesbians forming long-term platonic yet intimate relationships with one another, including conceiving and co-parenting their wonderful and creative children; and gay families through adoption, often including birthmothers or surrogates as active participants. These families cannot be boxed into a single narrative of the "normal" family form, and their diversity is both staggering and a source of pride.

I come from one of these complicated and creative families. I grew up in rural Washington State, geographically close but culturally far from Portland, Oregon. In some ways, mine was a stereotypical white nuclear family. My parents, high school sweethearts, were privileged to attend college, where they married and then returned to their hometown to raise their three children. Although my family was cash poor throughout my early childhood, by the time I entered middle school, we were comfortably middle class, and in many ways, strikingly unremarkable. In the mid-1980s, when I was eleven years old, that changed suddenly when my father came out of the closet. In the space of just a few months, my parents separated and subsequently divorced; my father moved to a townhouse only nine blocks from our family home, and he partnered with the man I would come to know as my stepfather. Our family became politicized; we were now the Other in our town, by virtue of my father's gayness, my stepdad's Blackness, and my family's ongoing commitment to one another in spite of divorce. My parents' commitment to each other never wavered; they remained intimately (though platonically) connected even after the divorce, communicating to their children that family meant something much larger than simply the institution of marriage.

Over the coming years, my father and stepfather separated, and my dad moved from our small town to Portland to live in closer community with other gay people. He bought a house, partnered again (and then again, and then again), and although he and my stepfather were no longer romantically connected, they continued to live together and support each other financially and emotionally. For the rest of my father's life (he died of AIDS in 1995), my three parents demonstrated the intimacy, commitment, and creativity of family, in spite of being entirely platonic in their relationships with one another (in fact, all three had romantic others in their lives during this period).

In the year following my father's death, my stepfather decided it was time to know his HIV status; he had postponed getting tested because of his fear for the stress it would cause our already taxed family system if he received a positive result. He did test positive, and when he looked into his options for health insurance at that time, he learned that he would not be covered due to his HIV status; he was left with a diagnosis and need for treatment, but no means to access it. Meanwhile, my mother (who was nearly nine years into a committed relationship) learned that her insurance policy would provide coverage to her legal spouse without a health screening. One year after my father's death, we drove to Reno, where my straight mother and gay stepfather were married for the purpose of health care; my mother and her straight male partner simply agreed that family needs took precedence over their desire to marry. Many years and health care policy gains later, my stepfather received coverage of his own and no longer needed to rely upon marriage to confer that benefit. He and my mother divorced, and my mother and her partner finally married after nearly eighteen years together.

Along the way, from the time my father came out of the closet to the time my mother and her partner were finally married, our family continued to queer in new ways. We became an informal foster home for neighborhood youth whom the child welfare system would have served had it existed in any real sense in our part of the county. My grandmother moved into our home, and my mother's sister and her children moved from Texas to provide care for my grandmother as her health declined. Meanwhile, my mother and younger sister moved *out* of our home and *into* my father's Portland home to share home care for him during his death. At the same time, as a college student, I spent the week caring for my lesbian best friend, who was dying of cancer at age twenty-three, and drove to Portland on weekends to provide relief for my mother, sister, and stepfather in caring for my dad.

I share this narrative not only because I am proud of what my family has accomplished and how our experience illustrates different ways queer people have and continue to family[ii]. I share it to destabilize the notion that gay marriage will demonstrate the normalcy and "just like you" character of gay families. I came out when I was sixteen, confident in the acceptance of a family that celebrated its oddity, even in the context of bigotry and ugliness modeled daily by the town in which we lived. Growing up, my family *was not* just like any other family, as we were reminded daily. We did not fit the established templates for relationships (for marriage—or divorce, for that matter—or even of what adult sibling relationships entail). Functionally, we disregarded conventional meanings ascribed to our relationships; as queer families always have, we defined ourselves on our own terms. Marriage was not the marker of legitimacy for our family. It was a political tool, an instrument we used when we needed to, but not the indicator of our love or commitment to one another. Coming from that family, steeped in these values of creativity and commitment, I have now formed a queer family with new twists.

We are complicated, my current family. At our most basic level, we are a family of four—three adults and one child—living together, related in a variety of ways, deeply committed to one another and intimately connected, but without conventional language to name us. My family today includes my partner (with whom I am romantically intimate), his sister (with whom I am not), and our five-year-old daughter, whose birthmother chose us to be her parents and with whom we have an ongoing relationship. My daughter and I are white; my partner and his sister are Vietnamese. Three of us are Jewish and one is not. We live together in the same home, our finances are entirely interdependent, and our emotional commitments run deep—all circumstances I hope never change. My partner's sister is not a parent to my daughter, but in name only; we have no term to describe the depth and intensity of their relationship. Likewise, she and I (and she and her brother) are intimately (if platonically) connected. I cannot imagine my home without her there, and again, we have no term to adequately name this connection. We are surrounded by my mother and her partner, my siblings by birth, two sisters by choice, and a complex constellation of other adults who support, affirm, and bolster us—they, too, are our family, and I struggle to find a title for these bonds. We are not merely close friends, we are kin, as clarified by Kath Weston in *Families We Choose: Lesbians, Gays, Kinship*.

My family is most certainly not "just like everyone else's." In restaurants, when my whole family is present, my daughter's two male parents are routinely ignored by waitstaff who—with all the best of intentions—ask my sister-in-not-law what my daughter would like to eat. They assume she is the parent because, after all, our dominant social norms suggest that the presence of a woman in the company of a child renders her that child's caregiver. Legalizing same-sex marriage does not address the sexism embedded in this taken-for-granted assumption that women are made for motherhood in a way men (even two of them actively parenting together) are not assumed to be fathers by default. Nor will it resolve the implicit racism I see in the faces of fellow passengers on public transportation, as they struggle to understand which two adults in our family created our blonde, fair-skinned white daughter; was it the two Vietnamese people who look a lot alike (my partner and his sister)? Or the Vietnamese woman and the dark-haired white man? We remain a mystery, a curiosity, out of the inability for people to fit us neatly into a tidy social template of family (signaled by racially matched married parents and their biological children).

I watch my five-year-old daughter explain to her blank-faced health care provider that "not all boys have penises and not all girls have vulvas," and I realize that same-sex marriage will not help my child navigate a world that still denies the trans* people in her life full recognition or even the right to name their own bodies. Nor does it help her to see her family reflected in her elementary school's curriculum—her same-sex parents ("Daddy," which most people understand, and the Vietnamese "Ba," which they do not), her aunt (who uses "Cô," rather than "Aunt"), her birthmother, her five grandparents (three of whom are white, one Vietnamese, one Black, and none biologically connected to her), and the host of other adults (all of whom are actively involved in her upbringing) surrounding her day in and day out.

I think about my own extraordinary privilege, to work in a university, to take classes for next to no cost—and how that privilege extends to members of my family (spouse or children). Same-sex marriage, however, will not allow my sister-in-not-law to access this benefit because she isn't family *enough*—in spite of us living together for the past six years, entirely financially and emotionally interdependent. The marriage movement also will not help other people understand that our occupational worries cannot be resolved by just getting a job elsewhere (a common recommendation from peers, given our class, educational attainment, and sector of employment). Our family form requires that for one of us to relocate, three jobs must be waiting.

Of course, in many ways, these are good problems to have. Coming out thirty years ago as a gay man with three children, these are problems my father would have loved to be able to claim. He faced active employment discrimination, threats of physical harm, and more, that I have never feared in the same way. Considering my queer peers who experience homelessness, struggle in poverty, are incarcerated and subject to inconceivable violence inside those walls, fear deportation, navigate health systems that deny them care without psychiatric diagnoses, and encounter interpersonal and structural racism every day, these problems fade into near insignificance.

But that is precisely the problem. I am, in so many ways, one of those gay people most like those driving the marriage movement. I am college educated. I am white. I am comfortably middle class. I am accustomed to being heard when I speak and finding ways for my needs to be met when I communicate them. I am in a relationship with someone I could call "husband" if the law allowed. Yet even for me, achieving legal same-sex marriage does not solve any actual day-to-day concerns. It simply solidifies as valid one form of relationship, of family, and by virtue of claiming recognition for that one form, it pushes the rest of us further out to the margins and leaves us further behind. Poly families, drag families, multiple couples co-parenting the children they created together, trans* and genderqueer families, poor queer people with no access to the assets marriage promises to protect—will still struggle for recognition of their families and relationships, and our communities fracture even more. None of this is intentional on the part of individual gays and lesbians who want recognition for their relationships; I am under no illusions and make no accusations that they deliberately pursue assimilation, or that they hope to deny diverse queer families the recognition they also deserve. Nevertheless, this is how the politic plays out.

So what do we, as a community, gain when we chase access to traditional marriage in the name of equality? What do we lose? Who gets left behind as we march toward the interests of a select few who have the luxury to be worried about inheritances and visitation (but less about employment security, immigration status, violence, or poverty)? When I voice these concerns to my friends and colleagues, I often hear, "Yes, but it's a step. Those other things can be next. We have to start somewhere." I question, however, how and why we came to decide that *this* is the place to start, with the interests of those people who for the most part already stand nearest social acceptance. Those closest to the mainstream will benefit, and the others? They remain on the margins, and indeed, those margins will have been pushed further out. Codifying marriage as the legitimate form of queer relationships as it has been positioned—parallel to heterosexual marriage—actually restricts the diversity of queer families rather than opening it for further future gains. When our "equality" is predicated on marriage, those of us for whom marriage is neither desirable nor helpful will be even further from that goal.

The pursuit of same-sex marriage, in the guise of equality, is not a starting point; it *is* the point. It is the point where we turn a corner, and if we turn in the direction we are now facing, toward recognition only through the rhetoric of sameness, we actually move further from inclusion and true equality. We move away from affirming a rich diversity of family and in favor an increasingly narrow interpretation of "legitimate" relationships. Those in our community—in all communities—who want to marry should certainly be able to do so. Their relationships, *and all others*, should receive validation and recognition, or none should. But "marriage equality" is not a victory, not even an initial one, if it comes at the expense of other queer families, my own included, which are deliberately and deliciously *not* like everyone else's.

Notes

[i] I hesitate to use "LGBT" here out of recognition that I seldom see my bisexual or trans* friends and colleagues on the front lines of the gay marriage movement, let alone included in any meaningful way by the mainstream movement or organizations that claim to represent them.

[ii] Thanks to Terry Boggis for introducing me to the idea of "family" as a verb. Family is what we *do*, not only the people with whom we do it.

Pamela Helberg

Holding Hands in Pocatello

Somewhere between turning three and turning fifty, I lost touch with being comfortable in my own body. I grew up in a family, which for the most part, at least early on, indulged my being a tomboy. They may have forced me into poufy dresses and given me the obligatory home perm for special occasions, but they recognized how much pleasure and comfort I took in being in cowboy boots and jeans, in being allowed to play in the dirt with my brother's toy trucks, and running around our house with my toy guns in their plastic holsters strapped to my waist. We lived in a logging town, forty-five minutes east of Seattle, on a ramshackle farm, and my gender nonconformity did not seem to be an issue. I had a boy's model bicycle, a BB gun, and I tried out for the Little League team. My parents were incensed on my behalf when I didn't make that team—I could run, throw, and hit as well as, if not better than, most of the boys—but in 1974, girls did not play Little League baseball.

I was eleven when I realized a great gulf yawned between how I felt and what society expected of me as a woman. At the edge of puberty, I was expected to step away from the boyish play that made me happy and move toward feminine pursuits that felt awkward and foreign. Instead of fighting for a spot on the baseball team, I was to just lay down my bat and ball and put away my mitt. Didn't I want to join Rainbow Girls and learn to sew in 4H? I did not, but there didn't seem to be a choice. That was what young women did. People saw in me a girl, a young woman, and it did not make them happy that I dressed and acted like a boy. It didn't matter that I felt more complete in short hair, jeans, and sneakers than I did in dresses, heels, and makeup. It didn't matter that for the first ten years of my life I had been indulged and allowed to cross gender lines. Once puberty called, I had to play by a new set of rules. I began to internalize the not-so-subtle messages of peer pressure.

While my friends suddenly found boys fascinating, I loathed them. Boys I had once played with morphed into strange creatures, aggressive with an unwelcome sexuality, ripe with innuendo. I couldn't get far enough away from them. Simultaneously, I longed to be closer to my girlfriends or to our gym teacher. I knew better than to speak of my longings, and I worked fervently to hide my true feelings, to feign interest in the latest teen idols, to pretend to enjoy myself as I went on dates with boys who pawed at me, and to breathlessly recount these adventures with my girlfriends at sleepovers. I started shopping for clothes in the girls' section, and gave up my comfortable jeans and baggy T-shirts for high-waisted jeans and clingy blouses. I learned how to apply mascara and eye shadow. I curled my bangs. While my outward appearance screamed straight, and my new teenage body, in its tight, new clothes, had no trouble attracting male attention, inside I was still a tomboy. Inside, strange new yearnings blossomed. Thus grew the divide within me, between the self I presented to the outside world and the self that lived surreptitiously inside me, coming out only when safe.

There were so many fronts on which it did not feel safe to be the real me. Having grown up in a strict fundamentalist church, being safe meant being saved. Being saved meant accepting Jesus Christ as my personal lord and savior, which meant constant vigilance and living in fear of eternal hell and damnation. When I discovered that there was a name for my unspeakable feelings toward women, that I was a lesbian, well, that was antithetical to being a Christian. I could not be both, though for a time I tried. A time during which I had to continue to deny my true self for fear of being shamed and cast out of the community.

Half a lifetime of therapy notwithstanding, I still carry all of that shame about not belonging and of being different with me. I carry it as a great and whirling anxiety as my wife, Nancy, and I travel in our Jeep from our home in Bellingham, Washington, through eastern Washington, eastern Oregon, and southern Idaho, on our way to a family wedding in Wyoming. It does not matter in these moments that same-sex marriage is legal in thirteen states, including ours. It does not make one whit of difference that the Supreme Court of the United States struck down the Defense of Marriage Act, or that they threw out Don't Ask, Don't Tell.

Nancy has a habit of calling me "honey" when we are out and about. She likes to grab my hand in public. These are endearing habits when we are not someplace like Pocatello, Idaho. Her innocent endearments become invitations for ridicule and perhaps death in my mind when we stop for breakfast at a local diner. By the time we finish our enormous breakfasts, I have overheard enough conversations about hunting, conservative local politics, and wishing the president dead, and my fight-or-flight responses are on full alert. My nerves snap and crackle, and I can't wait to leave town. I'm glad we won't be getting a hotel room and asking for a single king-sized bed. I walk quickly to the Jeep, dodging Nancy's attempts to touch me. I do not want to hold her hand in Pocatello.

We drive a few hours more, a blizzard on Teton Pass hiding the enormous granite peaks for at least the day. Maybe it's just the falling snow, but Jackson feels friendlier. The woman at the front desk of our hotel greets us enthusiastically. We have a heartfelt bitch session about the government shutdown and the closure of Grand Teton National Park and what it means for her business, and her customers—particularly the ones who have traveled internationally. We assure her we are happy to be there for a family wedding, shutdown or no, and we settle in nicely. Our room has only the one king-sized bed and she doesn't bat an eye. We even hold hands briefly here and there as we wander the town. We visit the famous Million Dollar Cowboy Bar, where patrons pony up to the bar on actual saddles. Definitely a tourist joint, it doesn't feel so friendly, though it is difficult to determine why. Is it that we are decidedly not feminine cowgirls, cute, skinny, and out for a good time? That's where my head always goes when I get shitty service. We sit in the saddles long enough to order, move to a more comfortable table to finish our drinks, and then on to a more friendly local bar recommended by our hotel hostess.

Being on display as a couple, outside of the comfort of our hometown, away from family and friends, takes an emotional toll. Trying to gauge reactions, monitoring my language and actions, and worrying about whether or not Nancy is monitoring hers—exhausting. I suppose I shouldn't care, should be confident enough to move through this world without giving a damn about what strangers think. After all, every day it seems like a new state is allowing same-sex marriage, and Congress is poised to pass further antidiscrimination legislation. But too many people are still dying at the hands of homophobes for me to relax and just be myself. By the time my brother and his family arrive in Jackson and we move into the house we will all be sharing for the next two days, I am more than ready to relax among familiar faces and family.

We all get dressed and ready for the wedding, my brother, nephew, dad, and me all in our jeans, Western shirts, boots, and hats. Nancy in her cowgirl outfit—her ruffled skirt and Western shirt with the longhorns embroidered on the shoulders, her new cowboy boots. I am far more excited about getting dressed for this wedding than for any others we've been to recently. I love my bedazzled cowgirl jeans and my new cowboy boots. I like being tall and how the boots make me swagger when I walk, and I am reminded of a photograph of me at my third birthday party. I am a redheaded toddler in a poufy blue dress, but over my dress I wear my Annie Oakley buckskin jacket with the fringes. I have a small cowboy hat on my head, and I've taken off my white Mary Janes to pull on my shiny new black cowboy boots. I am happy.

Now, however, behind the swagger lurks my constant self-doubt, the voice that always makes sure I know I'm not feminine enough, that I look too butch, too much like a boy, not quite right. As we drive to Teton Village, where the ceremony will be held among the golden and shimmering aspens and fiery fall cotton-woods, I fall silent, overwhelmed with worry and insecurity.

Nancy grabs my hand when we climb out of the Jeep and wait for my brother and his family, and my father and his wife, to de-bark from their vehicles and join us as we walk to the front of the (very upscale) barn. I let Nan hold my hand then, but I feel my confidence fading the closer we get to the venue, and when I don't immediately see anyone we know, no members of our large extended family, I pull away and drop her hand.

"So that's how it's going to be," she says, stopping on the sidewalk. "Really?"

I pretend not to hear and walk a little bit ahead, flooded with shame and hoping that either the ground will swallow me whole or that a posse of cowgirl lesbians might be waiting for us just around the corner. Of course neither happens. Around the corner I see only straight (as far as I can tell), normally attired wedding attendees—with suit jackets, dresses, and only the occasional cowboy boot. I want nothing more than to turn heel and run—to safety, to the familiar, to someone I've never been nor will ever be: a taller, thinner, more feminine, more socially acceptable me.

It does not matter in that moment that I am surrounded by people who love and accept me. It does not matter in that moment of panic that my brother is also wearing a cowboy shirt and cowboy boots and jeans and a cowboy hat. It doesn't matter that I came out to my family years ago and that my wife and I are as accepted and loved and as much a family unit as my straight cousins and aunts and uncles. All that matters to me is my obvious otherness.

I cannot flee. We are forty-five minutes early and will have to mingle and make small talk or stand awkwardly with each other. I silently curse that there is no alcohol before the wedding because I could really use a Scotch. I talk myself down from that internal ledge and try to see us as others might. I look at the individuals in the crowd and not at the crowd itself; feign interest in the barn and the surrounding grounds; and eagerly greet familiar faces as they trickle in. I remind myself that I am fifty years old, goddammit, and beyond caring what other people think of me and my life choices. I berate myself into behaving as if I believe that.

Eventually, I talk to enough people, drink enough wine, eat enough dinner, spend enough time to reinhabit my body. No one laughs at me. No one makes fun of me for being a lesbian. Only one person asks if Nancy and I are sisters. In fact, I relax and open up, and Nancy and I dance. We dance together, alone, with strangers on the dance floor, in the arms of family members, and as we dance a funny thing happens.

The wedding invitations had included RSVP cards to mail back. Each card asked for a song request—what song would we like them to play at the reception? Nancy told me to put down "Same Love" by Macklemore. I seriously doubted that our song would get played—partly because it's really not a dance song, partly because it's gay. But wouldn't you know it—about three quarters of the way through the evening, I hear those haunting, plinking piano notes summon us. I grab Nancy's hand and pull her onto the dance floor as I whoop and wave my hands in the air. My feet, unaccustomed to cowgirl boots, are killing me. We are the first ones out there, but not for long. My cousin and his bride wrap us in a huge embrace and thank us for making the trip. Strangers and relatives alike join us on the dance floor in what feels like an enormous celebration of love.

I wish I could bottle the feeling I had at the end of that night, wear it around my neck, and sprinkle it over me before I walk into new situations, because coming out isn't just a one-time event. Coming out happens over and over and over again, every day, every week, every month. Gay marriage may be marching across the United States, but we cannot legislate tolerance and acceptance, and we certainly cannot legislate self-acceptance. Don't get me wrong—I believe we are headed in the right direction, and maybe the generation of LGBTQ children growing up now will not experience decades of loathing by the general public. Maybe they will not grow up hearing their families and pastors and community members call them names like sissy or faggot or bull dyke, maybe no one will tell them they are going to burn in hell for whom they choose to love. Probably they won't get beat up or tied to a fence post and left to die. If they are lucky, maybe having same-sex marriage laws on the books will keep their parents from kicking them out of the house when they are teenagers. But, if history is any guide, legalizing same-sex marriage is just the first step in protecting the LGBTQ community from marginalization at best and active hatred at worst. America passed laws making abortion legal and outlawing segregation too, but having the laws did not guarantee anything. Thirty-seven years on and we are practically back to square one with women being able to get safe, legal abortions. The Supreme Court recently struck down the heart of the 1964 Voting Rights Act, and just upheld Michigan's affirmative action ban. Laws are mutable, and the courts often seem capricious. For those of us who came of age before same-sex marriage entered the cultural lexicon, we are going to need more than the legal right to take on the already shabby institution of marriage. If I am going to hold my wife's hand in a crowd full of strangers, I will need more than just the law on my side.

Emanuel Xavier

The Gay Revolution Will Be Televised—Viewer Discretion is Advised

June 28, 1969—In the early morning hours, police raided a mafia-run Greenwich Village gay bar named The Stonewall Inn that catered to an assortment of patrons including drag queens, homeless youth, middle class gays, and hustlers. Before the Stonewall riots, the queer community was far more mixed because everyone was disenfranchised and anyone could be arrested for illegal conduct. This meant a place like The Stonewall Inn had an easy mix of just about anything you could find under the rainbow.

During the '60s, in a cosmopolitan city like New York, it was illegal to serve alcohol to homosexuals, and it was illegal for two people of the same gender to dance together. Full drag was unacceptable. If you were not wearing at least three articles of gender-specific clothing, you could be arrested. Police raids on gay bars were commonplace and acceptable, but on this one occasion, the authorities lost control and incited a riot.

What was different about this one occasion? Some say it was the recent death and funeral of gay icon Judy Garland, and many were already sad and angry, but this was a spontaneous political expression, and tensions had already been building for many years. The birth of an underground movement had been brewing in large cities like Berlin, San Francisco, and New York's Greenwich Village and Harlem. Whatever the reason, the transition from the homophile movement to gay liberation was facilitated by this one iconic event. The gays fought back, the police were humiliated, and the modern gay movement as we know it began. As Allen Ginsberg famously said about the people at the Stonewall riots, "You know, the guys there were so beautiful—they've lost that wounded look that fags all had ten years ago."

Summer of 1987—At the age of sixteen, I became one of those homeless youth and hustlers at the West Side Highway piers. Almost two decades had passed since the Stonewall riots and I knew nothing about them. My only concerns at the time were a comfortable place to sleep at night, some money to buy food, and the fear of getting AIDS or being killed by a trick.

Marsha P. Johnson was a black trans woman who, during the Stonewall riots, had climbed a lamppost, dropped a heavy bag onto the hood of a police car, and shattered the windshield. This was perhaps the birth of a transgender activist, but I did not know anything about her. I did not know what her living situation might have been. All I knew was that she was always on Christopher Street in her tattered dress and funny-looking hats. She was friendly, if not odd, but underneath my breath, like all the other pier queens, I would simply make fun of her. I remember being told she should be respected as I rolled my eyes with contempt. Still, years later, when her body was found floating in the Hudson River after being brutally stabbed, I knew someone truly genuine and important had passed through my life.

Fall 2009—I was teaching a spoken word poetry workshop at Sylvia's Place, a shelter for queer homeless youth provided by the Metropolitan Community Church of New York. Sylvia's Place was created to honor the request of another Stonewall riots veteran, drag and transgender Latina activist Sylvia Rivera, on her deathbed. There were only approximately thirty sleeping bags and maybe two other shelters catering to queer homeless youth in a city where it is estimated there are about a thousand gay kids out on the streets.

Spring 2014—It is truly essential that we acknowledge that some of our children still end up homeless because they come out to their families in this day in age. In cities all over the United States. This defies the illusion that we are living in a world in which the only thing gay people have left to win is the right to marry. It is even more disturbing that, forty years after the Stonewall riots, we as a community are more concerned with which half-naked, muscled twink to reward for his beauty than those mostly kids of color who would do anything for some of the clothes missing from the covers of our magazines. Most fag rags feature gays in nothing more than swimwear and sunglasses. It would be great to think all those missing garbs could be keeping a homeless kid warm in the winter. Lest we forget, it was the homeless kids and the hustlers, who had nothing to lose in comparison to the gay stockbrokers and such who could be fired from their jobs if outed, that were crucial to the Stonewall riots.

Besides that we can now openly drink, dance, dress in drag, and choose our own gender, some other important things have changed since Stonewall. However one decides to label themselves within the queer community, we no longer have to hide with forced anonymity. Gay pride is rebelliously loud and joyously celebrated. We are courted by companies as consumers with disposable cash. With the internet, it is easier for youth to get information, meet others like themselves, come out, and be openly and proudly gay.

However, let us not forget there is still poverty and homelessness within our very own community. There are still gay teens out there disregarded by the queer mainstream because they do not own a pair of Prada sunglasses or have enough money to afford a gym membership.

The Stonewall Rebellion was about a community realizing that it could come together and fight against oppression. Most recently, our community came together to force the government to accept us as more than second-class citizens unworthy of our rights, making our relationships as significant and protected as everybody else's.

But let us not forget that Stonewall legends like Marsha P. Johnson and Sylvia Rivera end up homeless or die in poverty. It is a sad reality that as we move forward as a community, our true heroes are often being left behind.

Ariel Gore

We Were a Pretty Picture

Nobody wants to believe me when I tell them it wasn't safe to come out in the mid-'90s if you had an ongoing case in family court. And I'm not talking about some court in rural Colorado or Arkansas. I mean in the Bay Area. In progressive Oakland, California.

I knew a woman who'd lost custody of her kids over it. Everyone knew someone. And everyone knew someone who knew a few more people. It was both rumor and reality, and it just wasn't worth the risk.

Not that I cared all that much about my sexuality back then. I mean, I hardly ever got laid, and my "identity" was significantly less interesting to me than my groceries—and how I was going to get them. Mostly I wanted to identify as someone who could pay her rent and keep the electricity on all month.

I had straight friends who claimed they got married for the health insurance, but the woman I was sort of dating at the time didn't have health insurance, and I didn't have health insurance, so it wasn't like we were missing the opportunity to lift each other up.

If feminism had taught me anything by then, it was that I'd do my own heavy lifting.

On weekend mornings, when we didn't have our kids, my other half-closeted single-mama friend and I used to wake up before dawn. I'd knock on her door three times. She'd make the coffee. And then we'd head down to the family court building and tag it, gently, with red spray paint:

MISOGYNY: LOOK IT UP, STAMP IT OUT.

My queer friends now would probably accuse me of perpetuating violent language with the "stamp it out" part of that graffiti, but my other half-closeted mama friend and I *wanted* to perpetrate some violence.

We were tired of being threatened by our exes, fists through walls, pushed up against doors, their hands leaving marks that no cops or mediators or judge cared about. "Look," my chino-wearing family court mediator once said to me, "he's never maimed your child. If he's never maimed your child, his temper isn't on the table as a child custody and visitation issue."

Funny, because my "lifestyle" was on the table.

I denied the "lifestyle" accusation by omission, by staying silent.

I didn't feel much like talking right then anyway. I was thinking about that word, "maimed." The mediator hadn't just said "hurt"; she'd said "maimed." She was an officer of the court in the county of Alameda, in the state of California, and she'd said it herself:

For all intents and purposes, violence against women and children was legal and permissible as long as the physical marks it left weren't permanent.

Violent language.

Tagging that building with MISOGYNY: LOOK IT UP, STAMP IT OUT was the only violence left to us. We'd take it.

And it wasn't like that family court mediator was straight. When I saw her at the dyke march in San Francisco, she averted her eyes. As if she was fooling anyone in the courtroom—*with those chinos?*

I averted my eyes, too.

I wondered if she went along with the anti-child, misogynist, homophobic norm in family court just to fit in. I wondered if she felt the need to overcompensate for her chinos by saying that violence was cool as long as no one got "maimed."

Or maybe she really felt that way.

I was learning not to confuse sexuality with radical—or even reasonable—politics.

She was getting paid as a government employee. Maybe it was that simple.

She'd figured out how not to worry about her groceries.

When the first queer couple with kids I knew broke up, they didn't dare go anywhere near family court.

As much as those two hated each other in the heat of it all, they didn't want to risk the kids ending up in foster care—even temporarily—over "lifestyle" issues.

There had to be another way.

I suggested we convene a counsel of grandmothers to serve as a kind of DIY jury. The queers liked that idea. Finally—something they could agree on. But they managed to work out a custody-sharing plan before I got the counsel together.

I was jealous.

Imagine working things out—even with all the smashed dishes and sobbing it would take—outside the institution of family court.

As violent and impossible as my ex was, family court had made things significantly worse. Judges had empowered him in his patriarchal attitudes, clerks had let him off the hook when it came to child support, the court-appointed mediator had recommended unsupervised visitation even after he'd been arrested for having our three-year-old on the back of his motorcycle, and the county had given him an official visitation order that the cops said trumped my criminal restraining order and allowed him to sit on the front porch of my apartment building any afternoon he pleased.

Between lawyers and legal fees and court-mandated psychology sessions, I'd been charged thousands of dollars for the bullshit.

Folks from family court all preached "the best interest of the child." But it was just a racket—a lot of people making a lot of money by keeping the exes as bitterly engaged as possible.

"That was a good idea about the counsel of grandmothers," my queer friend told me even after she'd settled everything with her ex. "You know, I relied very heavily on my spirit guide to get me through all that."

Maybe I just need a spirit guide.

I imagined all the other queers' spirit guides looked like Xena the warrior princess or some little wood nymph.

I lay awake in bed at night, hoping my spirit guide would appear to me.

I imagined Glenda the Good Witch suddenly illuminating the darkness between my bed and my living room ceiling. But there was only the dark.

One night I decided to take a few hits of weed before I went to bed.

Sure, I worried about the random mandatory drug test family court could hit me with on any given morning, but I figured a spirit guide was worth the risk.

I'd heard I could just drink a lot of water before the test and piss inconclusive.

I lay down, good and high, and stared up at the ceiling.

Nothing.

My mind wandered from Glenda the Good Witch to the grad school article I was supposed to be writing on misogyny in family court. I had all the facts and figures, but I didn't know how to put it together without stories of the real and lived.

The women I watched, week after week, being called to task by some white judge for the dumbest shit while their deadbeat exes just sat smug.

I tried to stay focused on conjuring a spirit guide.

And then it occurred to me: Maybe my mistake was in assuming that spirit guides always showed up visually—like in the movies. I closed my eyes. Maybe my spirit guide would show up as a scent, a feeling in my body.

I breathed. The faint smell of, what was it? Jasmine?

And my body? My feet hurt.

And so it was. Hardly the Dianic dyke-midwife I was hoping for, but I figured you had to accept whatever spirit guide turned up.

Jasmine and sore feet would be my spirit guide.

It must have been right around that time—spring of 1997—the morning my phone rang early, *Unknown Caller* on the ID. I picked it up anyway. I hadn't smoked any weed for months. I could pass a drug test. I thought, *Bring it, bitches.* But it wasn't anyone calling from family court. It was an organizer from a famous national feminist organization—let's call it Famous National Feminist Organization. She wanted to know if I'd be up for a demonstration that weekend.

Sure.

I was always up for a demonstration.

They already had another woman who'd agreed to do it. The two of us would wear wedding dresses and stand out on the steps of the county building—in front of family court—and we'd have a faux gay wedding.

We'd be pronounced wife and wife and we'd kiss and the press would take pictures and we'd all have a grand time.

"All right," I agreed.

Why not?

My daughter could be the flower girl.

I met another organizer from Famous National Feminist Organization at a coffee shop in Berkeley. She wore a purple sweater, handed me a hundred dollars cash "for costuming."

I spent fifty dollars on an over-the-top satin wedding dress at the Goodwill on Broadway in downtown Oakland, the other fifty dollars on groceries.

The next morning, when I put on the wedding dress, I was surprised that it made me immediately horny. I'd never consciously fantasized about weddings or marriage. Where had the association come from? This wedding dress = sex = hot? What kind of terrible rom-com movies had gotten into my head? The royal wedding of my childhood—Charles and Diana—was the only time besides *Roots* we were allowed to watch TV. *Oh, what did it matter why?* I loved that hideous dress; never wanted to take it off.

I made myself a strong cup of coffee, poured my daughter a bowl of Cheerios.

Later, she'd stand by my side with the little bouquet of jasmine flowers she picked from the bush outside our apartment window.

The woman I married wasn't my type. She was wispy and straight and she instinctively wiped her lips just after I'd kissed her.

Still, we were a pretty picture in the newspapers.

It was just a few months later that I found myself in a court-appointed psychologist's office, the psychologist inching her glasses down her nose before saying it: "Ms. Gore, I understand that you were once married to a woman."

"Oh, no," I demurred, covering my mouth with a neatly manicured hand. "That was a just demonstration for Famous National Feminist Organization."

"Oh," the psychologist brightened at that, and smiled. "I'm sorry," she said, "I just had to ask, you know."

And I nodded.

"I do love the work of Famous National Feminist Organization," she assured me.

"I do, too," I said, and I smiled even though my brain was punching through the walls of my skull with all kinds of violent language.

Back on the steps of the county building, after the wedding ceremony was over and the press had packed up their cameras and my daughter and her friends played freeze tag on the cement expanse, a pretty butch woman in a tuxedo approached me. "You know," she said, "Famous National Feminist Organization wouldn't let me and my fiancée get married today." She motioned to a woman wearing a simple peach-colored dress. "They were totally femme-centric."

I thought about that.

There was an actual gay couple that wanted to get married.

And I'd been hired as a stand-in with my fake wife because we were, well, a prettier picture: two women in virgin-white wedding dresses.

The butch crossed her arms against her flat chest, righteous in her tuxedo and her lavender bow tie. And she was right.

Of course she was right.

What the straight girl and I had been a part of was staged and silly. A good femme spectacle for the press.

I didn't know what to say.

I stood there, all inexplicably turned on in my Goodwill satin wedding dress. My body hardwired by every media wedding fantasy I didn't even know I'd taken in.

My feet hurt.

The faint smell of jasmine.

"Oh, honey," I finally said, then realized how condescending I must have sounded but didn't know how to fix it. How could I explain that handing your family over to the mercy of the government was no happy ending? Was in fact a patriarchal-capitalist racket? I wanted to promise her a counsel of grandmothers instead, ungoverned broken plates, spirit guides that didn't look like anybody else's. I pointed vaguely to the county building behind me, to family court. Our MISOGYNY: LOOK IT UP, STAMP IT OUT graffiti had been whitewashed again. I shook my head. "You don't really want access to that place."

The woman stared at me, confused.

So I said it again, even though I knew she wouldn't want to believe me. "You don't want access to that place."

Jeanne Cordova

Marriage Throws a Monkey Wrench

Yes, I'm a Californian lesbian feminist. And now I don't know what to do.

I found our long road to marriage (1990–2013) deeply rattling for both personal and political reasons. The Supreme Court's 2013 decisions—to strike down Section 3 of DOMA and legalize California gay marriage—threw a perplexing problem into the personal lives and politics of lesbian feminists.

I came of age at the dawn of second-wave feminism—circa 1970—when women across America were waking up to the facts about the heteronormative chains of marriage. When women, myself included, began to realize how living isolated from their sisters and within the household of a single male was colonization. When women were afraid that men saw single women past twenty-five as "put on the shelf," unable to get a man, as man haters, or worst of all, as secret lesbians. When women felt they *had* to get married in order to be economically supported. And so we lesbians took up feminism and fought against the mandate of patriarchal marriage.

For thirty years, feminist activists—my peers and I—fought against the "M" word in courts around the world. In the 1950s and '60s as we grew up, we saw marriage as a truly heterosexual way of life that enslaved women. In my twenties, I saw and heard about many open lesbians, some of them friends, having their children taken away in divorce and custody court. Women who separated from husbands got the short end of the economic stick (close to nothing) when they divorced. There was no such thing as "communal property." Married women were declared "hysterical" or "depressed" because their husbands controlled them. Few women had access to birth control, so they were tied to their husbands—and their unplanned children—economically.

Yet in 2006, when I returned from living ten years in Mexico, I found that "marriage equality" had become the front-burner political issue in the gay and lesbian movement. I was baffled and outraged. Since when did dykes and faggots think so highly of the institution that we'd spent our lives fighting against? Escaping heterosexual marriage was a fundamental reason so many of us came out as lesbians or gays! (Exactly *how* the marriage issue became our foreground issue, I will leave to historian Lillian Faderman, whose forthcoming opus, *Our America Too: The Story of the Struggle for Gay and Lesbian Civil Rights*, traces the battle for marriage.)

I remained in my sisterhood-supported, joyful lesbian ghetto all the way through 2010, ignoring marriage and the raging battle around me. I wanted no part of it even though "marriage equality" had finally become legal in California for a brief window in 2008. I was politically against marriage despite the fact that two of my best butch pals—Jenny Pizer of Lambda Legal Defense, and Robin Tyler, famously one of the plaintiffs in California's Prop 8—were deeply involved, the former traveling from state to state fighting for our right to marry. On the opposite side, my close circle of lesbian feminist friends argued against it. One among them, Ivy Bottini, said, "We'll lose our identity as gays if we assimilate."

Yet my age wasn't helping. I turned sixty-five and was diagnosed with metastasized cancer; operations followed. My partner of twenty-five years didn't help my confusion. She said "let's do it" one day and "never" the next day. I wanted to "hold the feminist line," but I also needed to ensure that she, and not my large biological family or other assigned beneficiaries, would inherit my wealth exactly as my living trust outlined when I died. I could avoid the debate no longer; I had to reevaluate the "M" word.

For me, the first step was to recognize that feminist principles have changed the world around us—the women's liberation movement really worked. We changed the reality of marriage for women. The long years of marching for pro-choice causes and economic equality have indeed separated women from enslavement to our biology. In North America at least, women have broken the glass ceiling in that we can now become doctors, lawyers, and corporate executives—we can support ourselves.

According to Jenny Pizer, who has been part of California's radical shift in family law, "marriage is not what it used to be for women." Today in California, a woman is likely to walk out of divorce court with nearly half of whatever she and her husband owned as a couple. Lesbians are no longer de facto "unfit mothers." Child custody decisions are now rarely tied to lesbianism. Women today have largely freed themselves from being hostage to unplanned children; most have jobs or careers, and/or mandated child support.

The second step for lesbian feminists is to accept that we are now sixty years old, not thirty. And for many of us being sixty or seventy has come with health realities we never had to consider. Many of us have friends who are dead, dying, or being hospitalized.

The first time I was hospitalized, in 2008, my partner and I had to fight conservative, often Christian, nurses for the right for my partner to be allowed into my room, and to sleep overnight. Being opposed to the sexist term "wife," I tried the word "spouse" with my nurses. No recognition. I tried the word "partner" on a doctor. He replied, "What, your business partner? Your tennis partner?" We remembered stories of other hospice-bound lesbians. A Florida case where one partner died and her biological family swooped in to claim the house, the car, and all of their shared treasures, including the children.

All our tortured discussions about whether or not to marry have been a complicated process between me, my partner, and my lesbian feminist friends. It has been painstaking.

This year when I finally "popped the question," my partner responded with a crestfallen face.

"Aren't we already married?" she asked, referring to our real wedding—a lengthy 1995 pan-spiritual commitment ritual, which both of our biological and chosen families, plus one hundred fifty friends, attended.

"Well," I hesitated, "then would you get legal with me?"

"Sure," she said. "But we can't invite anyone, especially not our families."

"Why not?"

"They think we're already married. They'd be confused."

"I guess we'll have to have a stealth wedding," I concluded.

"What does that look like?"

A week later I was diagnosed with brain cancer, which nicely answered that question. A stealth wedding is hurried—guests included any close friend who showed up at our house the Sunday before I was hospitalized. We pulled our legal papers and welcomed fourteen close ones to a stealth "legalization" in the backyard.

Being a cancer survivor for the last six years, including three surgeries in the last two years, is making a profound impact on my life. These factors tipped the balance for me. No matter one's will, no matter the intricacies of trusts and other documents one has created to protect one's partner, my politically motivated re-evaluation of what "marriage" means today for women, and my hospitalizations, showed me and my partner nothing trumps a marriage license.

We took the plunge in late 2013. My last trip to the hospital was very different, and I couldn't help bragging. "Oh, she's coming with me," I told any staff within hearing distance. "We're married. Gay married!" Most of their faces lit up like they'd seen us on the news. Others had the decency to pretend-smile.

Perhaps "principle" is why an older lesbian feminist couple recently quipped at a dinner party, "Oh, by the way, we got married a month ago." With some embarrassment they revealed they'd also had a stealth wedding! They'd simply gone to a registrar, pulled the paperwork, paid twenty dollars for the court's witness, and enlisted a judge to pronounce the words. When I asked what made them take the plunge, one of them said, "I couldn't live with worrying…what if my partner died in a plane crash in a state that didn't recognize gay marriage…and they refused to let me in and take charge because I wasn't 'next of kin?'" What if?

The question is magnified if, at the end of one's life, a lesbian has accumulated enough wealth to make a significant difference to their surviving spouse. Realizing that the results of one's entire life's work could be passed on to the State or an unknown relative is a game changer.

I had to ask myself, why not take advantage of the privilege that I, as a lifelong activist, and others had won for our LGBTQ community? Sure, I am still angry that the State has the right to validate my partnership. Sure, I'm still angry that the State discriminates against singles and queers in red states. Yes, I hope the LGBTQ community continues to evolve into what I call a "single payer" state of marriage; under this *Grey's Anatomy*-inspired system everyone would have a "my person"—an individual who has pledged to care for you and be cared for by you. In the meantime, I mean to take advantage of each civil right hard won.

And yet, grave concerns still plague me politically. As the last decade has brought unprecedented success to "marriage equality," I remain worried that my LGBTQ movement has adopted a single issue as its primary battle song. History teaches us that any social change struggle that adopts a single issue as its focus eventually peters out when that single issue is won or lost. A look at the first and second wave of women's liberation demonstrates this lesson. The first wave, the suffrage movement (1880–1920) when women pursued the right to vote, began with the then-radical notion that women were held in legal economic bondage like chattel by men. A single woman couldn't vote or hold property in her own name. (Similarly, African Americans were, despite the Civil War, still in Jim Crow and economic bondage to white society.) After decades of struggle on multiple issues, the suffragettes finally settled on one single issue, winning the right for women to vote. And yet when women won that right in 1920, that first-wave movement dissipated. The masses of marching women went home. The first wave died. Women had to wait two more generations, until 1966, to return as the second wave, the women's liberation movement of modern times.

In its early radical stages the rise of feminism fought against multiple issues, the entire patriarchy. We decried marriage and the heterosexual presumption that all women are born to serve men. We focused on planned parenthood, birth control, and abortion. We went after rapists, making sexual assault a real crime with real jail terms. We spotlighted all forms of violence against women. We lesbians, many of us the early feminists who led NOW and other top feminist organizations, demanded and won the right to see lesbianism as a feminist issue. We fought for equal pay and to break the gender ceiling in our jobs.

But finally, after a decade of struggle, second-wave feminists began to highlight one single issue—the Equal Rights Amendment. Years later, in 1982, the ERA failed to pass in the necessary thirty-eight states. In other words, we lost. The millions of marching women of the 1970s and '80s who had gathered to fight for the ERA went home. The second wave dissipated, becoming thousands instead of millions.

As an activist, I fear the same thing is going to happen to the LGBTQ movement in the near future. As we have adopted the single issue of marriage equality, many more radical and more necessary issues—like the right to hold a job while being openly gay—have been pushed aside. As Richard Kim further said in *The Nation* in 2014, "Yes, some woefully underfunded groups still fly the flag of liberation, but the movement—and the culture—swims almost entirely in the mainstream."[i] We queers are told the tide has turned, gays are free to get married. As my metrosexual brother informed me, "You gays are normal now. No more of this 'outlaw' stuff."

Yet in 2014, a year after the Supreme Court struck down DOMA, and a year in which several major gay writers call the end of the gay civil rights movement, the new mayor of Latta, a small town in South Carolina, fired the woman who had served as the town's Chief of Police for twenty years—because she was a lesbian.[ii] Later that year, the dead bodies of two Texas lesbians were found in a dumpster where the femme woman's enraged father had shot and dumped his daughter, and beaten her butch lover to death. Months later, a black transgender woman walked down Hollywood Boulevard in the liberated state of California and was badly beaten by young het Latino thugs looking for a thrill.

How could such things still happen? We are "free" to marry.

Notes

[i] Richard Kim, "Close Down the Gay Movement? If it's all about handing out gold stars or scarlet letters to CEOs and celebrities, then I'll pass," *The Nation*, (May 5, 2014).

[ii] The police chief, Crystal Moore, was reinstated in June 2014 by Latta's town council.

Francesca T. Royster

Changing My Mind

There's a photograph of my parents' wedding that I've kept, even though my father has twice remarried, and my mother has since sworn off marriage completely, choosing over the years to either shack up or live single. The wedding was held in my great-grandmother's powder-blue living room, in her house on Indiana Avenue located in Chicago's south side. It's 1962, before I was even born, and my sister is just a small sea creature living inside the bride's belly. The photo is a little off-center, as if it were taken slightly from above. My mother and father are standing close and leaning forward, laughing, looking as if they are about to blow the candles out on a cake. They look like they've just jostled each other, flirtatious, or like they've just found themselves at this wedding, and somehow, one of them is wearing a suit and the other a veil. They look like they are used to doing things together, facing the good will and hope and high expectations of all of their relatives, who have assembled in their best clothing there in the dining room. They look like they like each other very much. My father is wearing a white tuxedo with black trim, his hair cut very close to his scalp with a part shaved into one side. His cheeks and forehead look very smooth. My mother's cat eye glasses are a little askew, and she is smiling widely, showing even her top set of teeth, which she never does because she thinks they are too crooked. Her hair is pressed into a flip, a style that she'll abandon for her own natural kinks just a few years later. I don't know who took this photograph—maybe another relative, maybe my great-grandmother herself—but, because of the poor exposure, everyone else and everything else is blocked out. It's just them, suspended in time, laughing.

I've thought of myself as "not the marrying kind" for a long time. Even before I knew I liked women, I was queer on the idea of marriage. At first I thought that what scared me was the idea of walking down the street and being seen as a couple *only*, my own self disappearing. That's what's captured for me in the phrase, *man and wife*. But as I look deeper, I see that what scared me—what still scares me—is the idea that you can live day by day with someone, entangle your life with theirs, let your body, your goods, even your ideas and dreams meld with theirs, and be wrong. Remembering my parents, I chose to turn away from that prospect of loss, and to invent, instead, my own methods of connection. But to my own surprise and joy and fear, I'm deep in it: house, child, life partner, risk. And what's more, the home that I thought I lost as a child is still with me.

I'm seven years old and my sister Becky and I are riding with my dad from our home in Nashville to visit his new home in Albany. As we move from Tennessee northward, red and orange and blue-gray cliffs of clay and limestone hug the highway, jutting out from beneath the buildings and concrete. I want to slow the cliffs down as they whip by us, like I want to slow down the whole trip. I want to take the orange stones with me, keep them, even though I suspect that they are in the category of things that can't be kept, or even touched, like baby birds that have fallen out of their nests. But when I ask if we can stop to see them, my father laughs and pulls the car over to the side of the road. My father, my sister Becky, and I empty out the paper bags that hold our car snacks: popcorn, red pistachios, and Planter's peanuts, and file out as other cars go speeding past us. My father keeps a lookout for crazy drivers and police cars from the bottom of the embankment as my sister and I climb the wall of stones. We select the smaller of the rocks, most of them still too big for us to carry, and put them in the back, along with our suitcases, and joke about them as our treasure.

I love the drive from Tennessee through Kentucky and Ohio and finally into New York, and I love the beams of attention I feel from my father when it is my turn to sit in the front seat, sharing pistachios, listening to the mixed tapes that he has made for the two of us, of songs he wants us to hear. When I get home from our trip, I hold the red-orange cliff rocks in my hand, and listen to the first song on the tape my dad made for me over and over again, Willie Bobo's "Dindi," from his album *Lost and Found*. Like a secret code, like cracks of hidden crystals, the singer's voice, smooth and then rough, says out loud what I feel I'm not supposed to admit; Bobo's voice, and guitar, and his breathy rhythmic scats make the sadness that I keep hidden about my parents' separation seem paradoxically upbeat.

I think of the conversation in my parents' bedroom, how both my mother and father are crying along with us kids, how messy it feels, all of our faces wet and twisted with feeling. I make a joke to stop the tears: "When you get your divorce, will I still get my allowance?" We all laugh, and that will become the story that we'll all tell afterwards, forgetting how we all buried under that blanket of sadness. By the time Willie Bobo's song reaches its lines about the lover who's so lost he's a river that can't find the sea, I feel like howling. Instead, I mouth the words quietly up to the ceiling. I hope that my father chose this song because he mysteriously knew what I was feeling, and because he was missing me, too.

A year before they divorce, when I'm five, I start to get head-aches, adult-sized headaches, that make me cry and clutch my head on my nursery school cot. The teachers, Miss Dozier and Miss Mayer, ask me if everything is okay at home. I let myself cry, and tell them that I think my parents are getting a divorce. They laugh, and try to reassure me. One of the teachers rests her hand on my hands. Another strokes my temples. "Plenty of kids worry about that. And lots of times they're wrong. It's all going to be okay," they tell me. But I know that change is coming.

The morning that we leave my father, I wake to the feeling of dread and the smell of wet cardboard: sweet, dusty, a little like the smell of the first day of school and that aroma of chalk and bologna sandwiches at the bottom of the lunch bag. It's raining outside, and I see through my bedroom window that there's a moving van pulled up to our front door. The door is open, and a man carries a large, yellow Mayflower crate, which holds the top of our glass dining room table padded in a blanket, and my mother is following him. She doesn't have her bra on yet even, just her nightgown and an unbuttoned robe wrapped around her, because the moving van came early, or we overslept, and I feel embarrassed for her softness. I am wearing my Holly Hobby nightgown and I feel like crying, but I keep the tears tight in my chest. The men, muscled and tanned and loudly chewing Juicy Fruit, are loading all of our things, packed or unpacked, into the van, and my father is nowhere in sight.

My parents' divorce is for me like watching those Tennessee cliffs whip by from our moving car, an exercise in willing things to keep from moving, shifting, slipping, but which always falls out of reach. My father soon gets a girlfriend, Cindy, who keeps her hairbrush and clothes and birth control at his new apartment. She helps him rearrange his furniture from the way my sister and I did it when we helped him move in. My mother meets Pat the cop, a gentle man who comes over after dinner and lets me put his hair in barrettes, even though he wears a holster and, when he's not in our house, a gun.

Even the cassette that my father made me eventually wears down. Willie Bobo's voice grows slower and slower, until the tape catches, garbles, whines, and suddenly stops, a tangled mess of magnetized plastic. For a long while, I give up on the power of my voice to stop things from changing, and so I grab onto rocks and pebbles, shells and driftwood, jam them into my pockets, and later arrange them in neat rows on my windowsill.

Leaf and mud and minerals welded together through time. Sand and dirt come off as I rub them, and I like to imagine my own sweat and oils joining the history on their surfaces, maybe someday to be found by somebody else. The rocks have been around for thousands of years, longer than we have, longer than the Fisk University faculty housing where we had lived together for almost all of my six years; a red brick and wood building with walls thin enough to hear the neighbors.

The rocks have been around longer than my father's new place in Albany, too, a high-rise he jokingly calls "Menopause Mansion." He is very popular there—the residents eye him in his white painter's pants and snazzy caps, and he appreciates the attention. It's populated with older, unmarried women: women who never married, women who left their husbands for another life, and women whose husbands left them. And there are some women who aren't the marrying kind. There are only a few men that I see, and they seem to be not linked to anybody either. When we visit, we are the only children at the pool.

Sandy and I are the only two who can't fall asleep during nap time. Our teachers and our parents decide that we don't have to, that we can play in the space between the nap room and the main playroom, an alcove where the teachers can still see us as they sip their coffee and talk quietly together, while the other children sleep. The alcove has built-in, kid-sized shelves, lined with picture books and dishes, puzzles, and the things that we find on our walks around the neighborhood—wrinkled crab apples, the pods that fall from the magnolia trees that surround the building, pebbles, and twisty sticks. Sandy and I take the pods and pry the hard, shiny red seeds from their dark centers, serve them to each other in our own version of a house where neither of us has to be mother or father. Sometimes we take turns: one with eyes closed, the other rubbing an object against the sensitive skin below the chin, or at the small of the back, reaching beneath the shirt. Is it rough sandstone? The furry magnolia pod, its prickly tips catching slightly on the skin? Sandy's cheeks are soft and always flush. His hair is longer than mine and falls in ringlets below his shoulders. He smells like glue and the others tease him for that, but I like the smell—milky and acidic at once. Later, I will keep looking for that combination of fur and rough, soft and spike, boy and girl, milky and chemical, the space of the alcove.

Strange that in most of my memories of my parents, they are separate from each other, even before they were divorced. I remember harried breakfasts and dinners, and Christmases, of course. And going hiking, and on car trips all together. But mostly I remember them doing things with my sister and me, or occupied with their own things. I remember listening to music with my father in the living room, sitting on the cushions or going through his record albums: Celia Cruz, Potato and Totico, Eddie Palmieri. He plays the congas along with teaching English and writing poems, and music is his passion. I remember my sister and I going with him to the park to play his drums, and helping to carry his instruments. I remember bringing his lunch up to his study, while he wrote.

My mother is my constant companion in those preschool years. I do just about everything with her, so my memories with her are of everyday things. Eating apple peels as she makes a pie, playing on the floor in the kitchen as she washes dishes under a huge "Free Angela!" poster above the sink, taking a nap with her on the couch. She combs my hair just like hers, in big Afro puffs. She is gentle with the comb and patient, and she makes me laugh even as she pulls and tugs.

One memory of the two of them together—not bickering, not avoiding each other—stands out in my mind. There is a big thunderstorm and the electricity has gone out. It is in the middle of the afternoon on a Saturday. It is during those months when we start to hear the word *divorce* in the arguments between our parents. My sister and I have been so busy playing in our room that we don't realize how quiet it's become. We can only hear rain and the occasional thunder. We don't know where our parents are. I wander over to my parents' room. The door is closed, but I go right in. They are all wrapped up in the sheets and a big flowered quilt. It seems strange to me that they are taking a nap in the daytime. My father's arms and legs are curled around my mother protectively. My father is wearing his blue robe, the one we got him for Christmas, but my mother is apparently naked underneath, her small brown body curled up tightly beneath his. She sleeps with her hands folded underneath her chin. I stand there for a few minutes, taking in the smell of their room, sandalwood and just-washed sheets. My father's eyes open. He puts his fingers to his lips.

"Shh."

"We're bored. We want to go outside. It's stopped raining."

He whispers, "Yes, okay, okay. Your mother is sleeping. Stay close to the house."

Outside, it's sort of like a holiday. All of us kids in the neighborhood are there in open slickers and rain boots, and now the sun has come out and everything. The leaves on the mulberry bushes, the sidewalks, the metal gates that surround the housing complex are wet and sparkling in the new light. My sister and I play for hours, free from the distraction of parents coming to get us to take us shopping or to lessons or to clean our rooms. It is as if the cut electricity has stopped everything.

Trans*form: [from the Middle English *transformen*. Formed from the Latin *transformare*: trans: *across* plus *forma*, to shape.][i] To reach across time, to reshape a story changes more than the story. It changes you. You can feel it in your chest, the way it opens up. The way your lungs welcome the air again. A sense of ease around the shoulders. A sense of openness in all your parts: eyes, pores, the palms of your hands, the soles of your feet as they meet the sidewalk, moving you forward. A sense of possibility. A willingness to see and hear even the things that may rock you.

I've looked at the pictures of my parents for all this time but now I see them at the age I am now. Actually, they're even younger than I am—by twenty years. I've opened my heart up to a child and a partner now, loving them with all my heart, and with that, opened myself up to the future. I've weathered heartbreak, learned the bone-headedness of love, been that moth ramming herself against the lightbulb again and again. And I've found love, been anchored by her, made a home with her.

I've weathered these things, but I haven't done it all by myself. They've been there, my father and mother, sometimes together, mostly apart. They've watched me, beaming from afar, like The Superfriends. But mostly they've stuck their nose in, lectured and instructed, and offered unwanted advice. Hugged. Sent checks. Shared meals. Met my friends. Sat in my own house.

I come out to my mother in a red booth in the International House of Pancakes, in the heart of Chicago's Boystown, some time in the early 1990s. "I already know," she says. "I've just been waiting for you to tell me." My lungs empty with relief. I had put off telling her for a while, unsure how she would react to a queer daughter. My mother always had "her boys"—male friends from work and from the AIDS ministry at her church, companions who turned to her for empathy and guidance and fun. She loved to go dancing. But while my mother always talked openly about her gay male friends, the sexuality of her woman friends was left unnamed. Their queerness was quieter, more subtle in their codes, but I still recognized in some of them an affinity: lean, irreverent Billie, who sang like Minnie Riperton and spent several months on our couch after she left her husband. And Liz, with her tomboy's short, curly hair and high-top sneakers. In the year after the divorce, she'd have us over for dinner in her neat, uncluttered apartment. She'd sit my sister and I down with the TV, while she and my mother would talk and cook, laughing in low tones. My mother never told me that some of her woman friends were queer, and never said out loud how much they meant to her. Many slipped out of her life with no comment or observation from my mother.

For so many years, my most passionate friendships with my woman friends also went unnamed. We were loyal and sometimes jealous, too, crying and confused at our explosions of feeling. But sometimes there would also be silliness and companionship and great, unaccountable joy. I'd keep these deepest passions in the periphery of my vision, distracting myself with boys and school and politics, knowing what I felt but still unwilling to look at it directly.

I am in my first real professor job on the East Coast, and my father and I talk about my queerness long distance, over the phone. Our conversations are more like our debates about *The Color Purple* or *The Autobiography of Malcolm X*: intellectual, abstract, but pulsing with an emotion kept in check only by a thin skin of wit and good will. He fears for my loneliness, he confesses, and he worries that I will face violence for being queer, as well as being black and a woman. I don't tell him that I've already been followed close by another car down a twisting country road, perhaps for my Xena and rainbow bumper stickers, or that I make my department chair stutter and he won't meet my eyes. I've already experienced the violence of being all too visible and of not being seen, of being both outed and invisible.

When I move back to Chicago, I begin inviting both my family and my friends to my parties. For my forty-second birthday, I ask my father to DJ, and he comes prepared, with his stylish cap and the painter's pants of his youth, and an iPod and speakers, bursting with the music he loves. For a while, he works quietly by himself in the corner, surprising us with his combinations: funk and jazz and hip-hop and blues drawn together by basslines that stretch across decades. Women, in all states of queer, begin to mingle around him. They bring him plates of food and ask him about the music. Soon, he takes out his bongos and begins playing along with the music. He lets one friend try out a few licks, and soon he's showing a small group a few patterns, always the teacher. Afterwards, he says, "You've got great friends."

My father and I are sitting on the couch in his day room in the large house he's built with Phyliss, my stepmother. I've set up the tape recorder on my iPhone, and he's set up a video camera, the fancy one that we all chipped in to buy him for his retirement. Before the interview, he's made us both "Dagwoods"—Morningstar Farms soy burgers, cheddar cheese, lettuce, tomatoes, and hard-boiled eggs on raisin bread—the huge sandwiches that he used to make for us when my sister and I came to visit him in his new home. His once-round afro has been cut short and is graying, but he still has a respectable head of hair. His hands shake a little as he sets up the camera. Before we start our conversation, he films a test shot, and we check it to make sure that the camera is working. I can see in the miniature image caught in the camera how alike we are. We both have the same heavy eyebrows and unconsciously worried expression. We're both sitting with the same slightly off-kilter posture, haunted by sciatica in our lower backs. Both academics, we face the same occupational hazards and the same addiction to chiropractors. Our legs are crossed in just the same way, one toward the other. When one speaks, the other nods softly, head held shyly tilted, as if to say, "Go on."

I ask him about home—our home, together as a family for that six-year time that we were all together; his memories of his childhood home; his knowledge of my mother's household, since she's no longer with us to tell us.

"You all were both so young," I say. "Eighteen and nineteen. Mom used to say that you had to have Grandmother cosign the marriage license—that she was really married to her, too."

"Her house was a hell," he told me. "And so was mine. We shared that. When I was growing up, my mother beat me, called me by my father's name. The last time she tried, I caught her hands so that she would know my strength. I was fifteen years old. I had been working since I was twelve, sweeping and carrying boxes at the drugstore, and I had trained as a boxer. My hands were strong. I had to show her how strong I was. She told me to get out. She kicked me out. And your mother, your mother didn't feel safe at home.

"Your mother loved our family. She loved building a home together, making decisions about your schooling and your hair and what we should eat. We'd never argue about that—it was like we were of the same mind. Even after the divorce. She loved our family. She just didn't love me." He tells me this last line while laughing, rocking his legs open and closed. But I can see that his eyes are wet.

I remember the love letters that my mother showed me from my father when they were courting. They all started out, "My Cherie Amour." She'd giggle as she showed them to me, shaking her head at my father's foolishness. But she still kept them.

I wish that my mother hadn't died before I had the chance to fully create the queer life that I yearned for so long. Annie and I had only been together for a few months when my mother died, but she did have the chance to see us together, our comfort in one another. This comfort sustained me in the unmoored year after her death. Annie knew how to ask just the right questions to allow for the waves of sadness to come, to let me drift with them, her floating beside me. She is the first person that I've loved that I've joined with my blood family to share in all of the intricate pleasures and dramas: potluck dinners and car trips, layoffs, tiffs, bounced checks, and eventually deaths.

It's January 2012. The State of Illinois legalized civil unions six months ago. Gay and lesbian parents can adopt. Though some organizations, like Catholic Charities, refuse to serve us. This year at the ages fifty-five and forty-five, Annie and I are preparing to adopt a child. We've just moved into a neighborhood of small bungalows all built in the 1910s, and this house will become the place where we'll forge this new life. A dream, an experiment, an investment in the future, though making a household is also something so ordinary at the same time. We are inventing family and home, but we are also shaped by the history of this particular city and neighborhood: Rogers Park, on the north side of Chicago.

Redlining, neighborhood covenants, riots, foreclosures. We are two women, one black, one white, with hopes of raising a black child. Right now, as we walk through the neighborhood together, some might see us as lovers, but others might dismiss us as "just friends." Walking buddies, coworkers, even relatives. But with our child walking between us, the stakes will be raised. We will redefine family just by being together, by demanding to be seen by our neighbors. What will our future bring? How will our community receive our child, queer by association? What will be awakened by the change that we're creating, breaking the hard stone of history with the pressure of our loving one another, elements accidental and purposeful?

It's May 2012, and Annie and I are going to see our daughter, Cece, in the nursery at The Cradle, her adoption agency, for the first time. She is tall for a five-week-old, and when you wrap her in your arms, her legs hang over a little. Her arms are already outgrowing the terrycloth pajamas that they have her in, and when she sleeps she raises up one arm, a Black Power salute. We give her a bottle of milk and decide right then and there that we love her. We will be her family even if we don't get to take her home. After visiting her for two weeks and being told that she is ours, her birth mother decides that she needs more time.

For five grueling days, Annie and I sit with uncertainty. We analyze every sentence of the email from our social worker for signs of hope. We spend our evenings wrapped in each other's arms on the red velvet couch, eating animal crackers and watching episodes of *Friday Night Lights*, trying to breathe. We go for walks in our neighborhood, have friends over for tea. We read and write and talk and teach, the academic calendar not quite done for the year. We are told by Annie's therapist to chant the mantra "I don't know," but we decide together that need to wear our scarred, lumpy hearts on our sleeves. We need to believe in this family that we've envisioned together, to stubbornly commit to the "as if": that the life that we've imagined for ourselves will become ours.

We must have convinced someone, because Cece comes home to us. On a drizzly gray day in May, we drive the two miles from

Rogers Park to Evanston to pick her up from the nursery, our tiny Honda Fit packed tight with the car seat sternly fitted by Officer Diaz, who warned us that from now on our own legroom is irrelevant. We videotape ourselves on the drive, so that some day Cece can see us on that day and witness our magical transition from "free," unencumbered women to parents. As I watch the video now, it's clear to me that the transition had already happened. You can see it on our faces: we share the same wide-eyed, slightly stunned look, like we've just been lifted by a sudden, unexpected wind. As if we had been sleeping a long, long sleep and our blankets have been snatched away. Neither of us can stop smiling.

Notes

[i] Oxford Dictionary, "Transform," Oxforddictionary.com, http://www.oxforddictionaries.com/.

Casey Plett

The Days of the Phoenix and the Emerald City

1.

In the first months of 2003, on a weirdly sunny winter afternoon, in Eugene, Oregon, when I still thought I was a guy, I was walking away from my high school when I saw this boy and girl walking together in front of me. They had a mutely alternative look: they wore all black, but no patches or pins of the sort you usually saw on Hot Topic kids like me. They each had an arm wrapped around the other's side. Even from behind, they looked incredibly happy. Like anything could reject them in this conformist world, but nothing would matter, because they had each other. I was fifteen.

They were smiling quietly when I passed them, and I saw the girl had black eyeliner, and I think the guy had a small devilock. *Weird*, I thought, *I've never seen them before.* It was possible they weren't in high school anymore, but you usually didn't see kids like that stick around our side of the Willamette River; they went south to the quarter of town with the hippies and anarchists and record stores and shit. The part that everybody, as if by committee, had agreed was going to be the unquestionable face of our little city. Meanwhile, our part of Eugene looked like any generic suburb: malls, SUV window flags, etc.

When I came back to school for drama rehearsal, the two of them were cuddle-walking up the sidewalk again, as if they'd just been circling the block. This time we stopped and talked. Mostly the girl talked, and the boy and I were quiet. We didn't talk long, but she said to me, "Your shoes are different colors! That's so cool!" In sophomore year I wore different colored Cons. Orange on the left side, black on the right.

They really looked so happy. I felt very warm thinking about her liking my shoes, like that was some stupid window into being a part of what they had.

2.

A story of a very nice day:

It's September of that year, a warm morning, and when I get to school, my ex-girlfriend, Naomi, hands me a bag of her clothes, and I walk into the bathroom. I'm going to dress in drag with our friend James. For a joke, to shock people. It's Naomi's idea. She likes to get a rise out of people. And she knows I like to wear dresses.

In the bag are purple fishnets, a feathery pink negligee, a white camisole, clip-on hoops, and a short forest-green tartan skirt with a silky black sash in its belt loops (the part of the outfit I like most—it looks so casually sexy). I twist and zip and slip her clothes on and, while syncretic pools of peace and shame spread up my body as I do, I also don't really think about it. I press my hands down the sides of my body, then breathe and strut out of the bathroom. I'm in the drama hall, where all my friends are, and everyone hoots and giggles. Ever since I started theatre I've been slowly breaking out of my shy-little-boy shell, and for the first time I have all these friends. And I love that they're laughing with me dressed like this. We are a large school, and there are dozens of kids in drama, and I feel like I have a community.

Naomi drags me over to the light booth stairs, where Angela is going to put on my makeup. Angela is a painter and a backstage techie, a tall, unhappy girl with olive-green eyes. She's also a total smart-ass and incredibly, incredibly kind. She puts rouge, mascara, and lip gloss on me. "Hold still," she says, calmly and firmly. Then eyeliner and eye shadow. "Close your eyes."

I've watched Angela paint and apply makeup before. She becomes different; her eyes focus and she becomes quiet and intense. I like this side of her, working on me so tangibly. I like offering my face to her.

"Um, okay?" she says, when she's done. "You can open now?"

James is late, so I walk to class alone. When I do, the boys call me a faggot, but—unlike years ago—I'm just laughing at them now. I yell, "Maybe, so what?" and the girls point and whisper, but nothing much else happens. I feel wild and like I'm getting away with something. I sit down in econ class and someone says, "Why are you dressed like that?" and I say, "Everything else was dirty!"

That joke had been James's idea—who now comes into class late and slams his stuff onto an empty desk. His makeup and clothes are like mine, except he's wearing a men's top. "Shirt didn't fit," he explains over the class he has silenced.

Homophobia is a weird thing in our part of Eugene. It exists, and it's mean, and most queer kids don't come out until after graduation. Two years back, the school board voted on whether to fire a teacher who'd come out to her students; three years back, the whole state voted on whether to ban mention of "homosexuality" in schools altogether. (Both were voted down, but not by much.) And yet, right now, no one is really getting in our faces *that* much, and it dawns on me how amazing that is. And back in the drama hall, obviously, no one had cared. In the theater-dude crowd I've begun to run with, homophobia is almost becoming an old fuddy-duddy thing, something for football players and Republicans. Certainly it's wrong and awful. But moreover it's old and uncool. It goes in this huge barrel of stupid things you're supposed to make fun of, like Limp Bizkit or feminism.

James is part of this theater-dude crowd, this hilarious hyper kid. He eats wax paper from muffins. When a girl outside the drama hall calls the two of us fags, he screams, "I haven't been fucked like that since grade school!" (We get a warning from the principal that students are scared to walk through our part of the building.)

At lunch I weird out some skaters. They're walking through the drama hall when I come out of the bathroom. Later I think of the scene: they're gingerly stepping through one of the freak sections of school and then a six-foot guy in drag shoots out the side of the wall. Anyway, they're really startled. They yell this jumble of *WhatTheFuckWhatAFagGrossAh* and I collapse cross-legged on the floor and pull up my skirt and say, "Ohhhh yeahhhh!" They sweep past me, still yelling through the door that leads to the art wing, and I run out to the courtyard and motor around the side of the school to head them off. I see them through an entrance door window and I crash against it, smudging my face on the glass and yelling, "Fuck yeah, boys! You want some! Huh? You want some?" They shout more and they turn to an exit that leads behind the school and I start after them. I'm unbeatable. I'm human lightning. Nothing can harm me, and I do not feel hurt by any name I am called that day. I am suddenly so angry and righteous in a way I haven't really known, and all these memories are surging back, like through them I'm getting even with other boys: The ones who called me a sissy for my pink-rimmed glasses in first grade, who

lifted and threw Baby-Sitters Club books out of my hand in third
("That crap is for *girls*," they yelled), who scrunched next to me
on the bus in sixth grade and told me I was gay, gay, worthless,
gay, no one will believe you because you're gay. With boys who
shoved me to the ground, the boy who choked me on a snow hill
in second grade, the boy who drove his bike into me in sixth and
punched me on the walk to my door. And with the parents who
tried to fire our teacher—I'm getting even with them all through
my eyeliner and my clip-ons and my feathery pink scrim. I want
to inject my picture into their eye sockets, I want my fishnets en-
graved on their retinas, I want to sink my head into their bellies
and smear my makeup all over their innards. I am marveling that
no one has tried to beat me up yet, but I suddenly want someone
to hit me, because I want to hit back. I want to grind their masculinity into the ground. I try with those skater boys. But they just
run away. I almost follow them out behind the school. Instead I
return to the drama hall grinning, and like most of the day's grins,
a slice contains rage. The bell rings and most of the hall empties,
but I have third period free and nothing to do.

I'm driving down Gilham, during my free period, on my way
back to school—who knows what I've been doing. I'm singing
along to an electronica-flavored song in my black-sashed skirt
and white camisole, and when I pass a soccer field I have a vision of me as a girl, driving the car and singing. I see her from
the back, like I'm out of my body, as if I were in a car behind her.
I can't see her face, only her straight hair that goes down to her
neck, and her head moves slightly as she sings and tools calmly
down the street. She looks so instantly and arrestingly correct,
and it's like breathing electricity—and then she's gone.

Later that night, when my mom catches the traces of makeup
around my eyes and extracts the whole drag story from me, I hope
she'll laugh it off, like how in recent years she's laughed off the nail
polish, the band patches, the gelatin hair spikes from my freshman

year. But she's upset, in the quiet way only my Mennonite-reared prairie mother, who never raises her voice, can get. "Do you do this to get people to like you?" she asks quietly. "No," I say. "Are you doing this so people will think you're cool?" "No." "Do you really like dressing in clothes like this?" "Yes." "Were you sexually abused when you were younger?" "No." "Do you do this because you want to be a woman or other sorts of transgender issues?" "No, Mom! Jeez!" She is not angry, but she is upset. And I don't want to argue with her. I want her to laugh it off. I'm desperate for her to laugh it off. I'm angry and sad that she can't laugh it off. My mom can be nice, so very nice, and she has logged more single-mother years as my protector than any child could reasonably ask. I feel stupid and ungrateful. I just want her to laugh at her goofy son. I love being her goofy son. I assure her it means nothing, just playing around, just being silly. I'm desperate for her to leave me alone and laugh about it, and I act mad and hurt when she doesn't. "It doesn't mean anything serious, Mom, please!"

She lets it go. Shortly, my stepdad comes into the den, where I am on the computer. "I heard about what you did at school." He too never raises his voice. He speaks like a teacher who's exasperated about a math problem I'm not getting. "You're only doing this because you're insecure about yourself and your sexuality," he says. "That's not it," I say, in a small voice, and he says, "Of course it is!"

I go to my room and think about the girl in the car with the straight hair. I wonder if I lied to my mom. Maybe a little part of me does want to be a girl. But then that would make sense, I guess, since I like feminine things, and girls get to be feminine every day and nobody questions them. And even though I know in the cosmic sense that it is okay for a straight guy to like feminine things—well, the world won't let you do that all the time. So of course it makes sense I'd want to be a woman a little bit.

Well that's a funny tic, I think. *I guess everybody's got something to deal with.*

I go back to the den and write an entry in my LiveJournal. Part of it says:

> I dressed up in drag today. It was great.
>
> ...
>
> I was driving back to school during third, blaring Con-tact and singing along, and I felt very feminine and I liked it a lot. Maybe I do want to be a woman. Why not.

Two people comment. The first is the one openly gay girl at school. She says I'd make a pretty girl. I blush. I hope others will say the same thing. I really love that she says this.

The other comment is from my friend Brittany:

> **Brittany:**
> **(response)**
> why not?
> THIS is why not.
> :]

The "THIS" is a link. I click on it. It's a GeoCities site—an old-school personal home page. A picture shows up of a...trans-sexual? I think that's the word? She (he?) is large, looks mannish, and is wearing a frilly blouse. The page is for a support group she runs somewhere in the South. She's ugly. No, sadly ugly. Sad is the word that comes strongest to my mind. I laugh. Brittany's funny.

3.

Years before, in a small town, in a different country, when I was well into grade school and my mom was newly engaged, she and my stepdad decided to leave Canada and the prairie provinces where they'd lived all their lives, where, by their mid-thirties, they'd already acquired divorces and children, debt and sedans, snow shovels and degrees, dogma and kindness. They wanted to move to the States, so they took a map and, over months, they narrowed it down and down and down and down, until they come up with Eugene, Oregon. No snow, no zealots, a cultured college town. It wasn't big or small. And the Pacific Northwest, all the magazines were saying, was such a perfect place to live. My mom was newly a doctor and my stepdad was newly a traveling consultant, employed with an American company that could win us the visas. We moved in February, and on the drive the roads turned from ice to slush to rain. Eugene really was a nice city, and the best place, they thought, to finish raising their kids. It even had its own minor-league baseball team (I loved baseball back then): the Ems, short for the Emeralds, a takeoff on one of the town's nicknames, the Emerald City—the kind of name that shows up on tourist pamphlets but no one actually says.

I moved back to Canada a year ago, and now I'm in the same Winnipeg neighborhood I lived in with my dad as a kid—same kind of apartment, even live on the same street. It's a good situation. Funnily, it also wasn't much of a choice; the province had the best trans health care in Canada, and nothing in the States that I could get had any.

I'm asked a lot why I moved back here; I make up some half-true bullshit and try not to let the subtext fall out of my mouth: "Well, I had some health care issues, and Winnipeg's a good place for a writer—" (VAGINA). "I always liked this city and it was always sort of home—" (VAGINA).

Anyway. Lucky duck.

I didn't have an awful childhood up here, but I was a sad kid. I was lonely and bullied, either in the city with my magical and depressed impoverished dad or in a small, mean town with my kind but tired and overworked mom. I was a kid of divorce in a place where most kids' parents had married for life at twenty. And there was the whole femmy boy thing—I knew I was a freak and I felt like a freak and kids made sure I knew I was a freak.

By the time we'd moved to Eugene and I was in high school, all of that had blessedly changed—until, a year after I graduated, when I started to come out as trans, and then the freak stuff started happening again. At least when I was a kid, strangers had never threatened to kill me, thrown sandwiches at me from fifth-floor apartments, slapped my ass, followed me into stores, talked their way into my building and made grabs for my dick. Among other things.

After leaving Eugene, I lived as this genderqueer-type boy for a while in Portland, going to PSU and doing various flavors of check-me-out drugs, partying with high school friends and drifting in and out of both the closet and the hazy late-oughties scene (laden with gays and trans mascs, but not so much with trans women). I finally transitioned at twenty-three, after moving to New York City for graduate school. Most of my old friends didn't cut me out when I transitioned—and for that I was grateful—but a lot of them couldn't deal and had no idea what to do with me after—and for that I hated myself, then was sad, then just angry.

Eventually, I became angry at most of Eugene, and this time not just our little northern section, but the whole damn committee-voted face of Eugene—the faux-liberated, monolithically white, neoliberal GoreTex-washed town that would vote Democrat but couldn't look a homeless person in the eye, laud Obama then rant about immigrants, make a show about gay marriage (once it was safe to do so) but not wrap their heads around me.

When I came out at nineteen, my mom lowered her head and quietly said, "That's very disappointing for me to hear. I certainly consider those people on the fringe of society." (Like herself, as I'd suggest years later, on better terms, when she was divorcing in the land of the Mennos, decades past.) My stepfather said, "You are not going through anything millions of men for centuries haven't gone through! Being transgendered is like being obese, it is something I tolerate, but not something I condone or support!" (*Um*. A lot of things wrong with that statement.) "It just seems so solipsistic," my roommate said. (He was going to Reed College at the time.) "Do what you want, that's fine, but I'm not going to treat you like a girl," said my best friend. "You'd make an ugly-ass chick," said James. "Most transgendered people," said a friend's mom, a university doctor, "are very unhappy. And most of them regret doing it." That one stuck with me not only because I believed her authority and it helped delay my transition—what other examples did I have?—but also because this mom had loved that I'd worn dresses in high school.

And I never thought any of this was negative at the time, because how could any of us have prejudice? We believed everyone was equal. We'd all had gay friends for years. My mom and stepdad had this one lovely couple over for dinner all the time.

But when I did finally transition, after those years of agonizing and self-hate and fear, my stepdad said, "Wow, you know, if you had just walked in one day and said, 'This is who I am now,' I would've been like okay, you're out of my life," and I said, "Haha. Yes, that makes sense, I will remember that," and my mother, standing next to him, said nothing. He asked me to never come out to his dad, a kind old man with failing health who I am still not permitted to see, and probably won't until he is dead. My mother's father, with whom I'd been close as a child, who took care of me after my parents' divorce and also his own, stopped talking to me for a time, and when I told this to her, she said, "Huh. That's weird." By this time it was 2011, not 2006, and now my parents' friends were lauding them for being so accepting of my transition. As I'm guessing they still do.

I am glad my parents found peace leaving their homeland, as I have found mine by coming back. I wonder if perhaps an anchor for them, in that new, tolerant world they'd found themselves living in, had been the knowledge that there were still limits.

I get along with most of my family now. We are kind to each other, for which I'm thankful; there are just some things we don't talk about. And I'm blessed with many loving friends whose empathy has never wavered. It's odd, I suppose, that of the wide menu of things I can be mad about, that my anger energy—the seething, useless kind—tends to center around these minor aggressions from my past life in the Pacific Northwest. As opposed to, say, the major aggressions from, say, the whole damn world.

I think I had a lot of faith, as a teenager, that by moving here we'd escaped it all. A stranger might not have guessed it looking at me, but going to high school in Eugene, Oregon, was the only time in my short life I've been something close to normal. I went to proms, I played the saxophone, I acted in plays. I had friends, was rarely teased or bullied, took AP classes, got good grades. My parents bought a house, paid off their debts, purchased a second car. We were thousands of miles away from our poor, cold, fundamentalist origins. We had a warm, upwardly mobile middle-class life, the kind ensnared with security and hope and unshreddable love—the life that as a child I'd longed for so desperately and as an adult now feels distant and impossible to repeat. So what if I wore skirts or nail polish sometimes, or if our neighborhood still had its share of conservative jerks? We had the Beautiful New Liberal American Life unfolding. Like we were all going to be a new version of regular people. There were a couple of years in high school where I never wanted to do anything more but move to south Eugene and get a teaching degree. Grow a paunch and meet a girl. Drink beer and volunteer in the gardens. Take day trips to Portland and reminisce about Ozone Records before it turned into a yuppie A/V store, before the yuppie A/V store went out of business. ("God," I could be saying right now at the Kennedy School with my paunch and beer, "what's it now, probably the Fred Armisen Organic Cupcakery or some shit.") Go to the antiwar protest and donate money for the gay marriage ballot measure. Call grandparents who love you in the old country you left. Have health insurance that pays for what you need. Laugh at links of the fucked-up shit that friends send to you online.

4.

Earlier in 2003, in April, I go to see AFI in Portland at the Roseland Theater. *Sing the Sorrow* has just been released, but I still love them for the goth-punk band I'd fallen in love with on *The Art of Drowning*. Also, I have to be honest: I want to fuck Davey Havok so bad. I know, I'm not gay! Davey Havok is truly the only man I want to fuck. And, well—be. He just, he wears these shiny black zippered clothes and long black hair and eyeliner and nail polish—it's so sexy and pretty and beautiful, all at once. He's like an example for me. Like, "Look, this isn't all just for goth chicks, straight boys can do this, too."

I ride up to Portland with friends and we eat an extra-large sausage pizza from Rocco's in O'Bryant Park. I give half of it to homeless people before the boys I'm with say, "Stop, stop, stop, you're going to give it all away!" I buy a band patch at Ozone, across from Powell's. We go to Powell's and look at a first edition of *The Hobbit*. When we line up at the Roseland, it's rainy and cold. I only have my black threadbare sweatshirt with a big AFI patch sewn on the back, a black-and-white logo with wings.

While we're standing and shivering, I think about seeing my girlfriend the next day. We're always so awkward around each other. "Touch me," she sometimes says, when we talk about this. "I want you to touch me." And I try, I do, but I just can't; my body becomes lumber and my arms are like long bricks. I want to feel her touch, I do (she's so beautiful). Nights I dream about us curled in bed. So when she's in front of me, why can't I touch her?!

When AFI comes on stage, I'm right in front. Davey Havok crowd-surfs over me and *Oh my God, I feel his hair*. And his arms and his legs. He's wearing all white, and he feels electric. Like everyone around me, I scream along on every song, and most of the time I can't even hear Davey sing, but I don't really mind. I can hardly breathe and my neck is permanently craned and I can't move it anywhere else with how thick the crowd's bodies are, nestled into each other. A guy's arm gets around my neck; it chokes me for a few seconds before he moves it away; I don't think he even realizes what he was doing. I scream and I'm squished and I'm liquid and I'm lost. During the final encore, Davey walks onto the crowd and stands on our hands like we're a human floor. I'm right below the split of his legs and I look right up to see the crotch of his shiny black vinyl pants (he changed) and I touch his legs and his feet—but everyone's converging on both him and me, we're all trying to touch him, and I fall backwards, and people fall on top of me, and I fall on someone below me, and the crowd below Davey's legs is a three-dimensional drowning mass of shiny androgynous bodies pressing and pulsing on me and pressing pressing touching in soft gleaming black clothes and flesh void touching wrap me I can't breathe touch me falling touch me I can't breathe I don't I can't care touch me I can't breathe touch me wrap me press me shit—

The encore ends. The music stops. I realize I am about to pass out unless I get fresh air, like *now*.

I push through all the bodies daze-walking to the exit and take off my shirt in the rain and slump against the wall. It's cold and miserable and my body is shrieking but I'm more alive and in my body than I've ever known. It's about half an hour before I'm breathing normally again.

5.

It was before the show started, wandering the floor, that I ran into the boy and the girl from months back, the ones in black who were cuddling while they walked. It was the only time I ever saw them again. We recognized each other, the girl and I squealed, then she bent over and inspected my feet. Her face came up scrunched, almost hurt.

"Your shoes match ..." she said.

I wanted to wear all black that day, for AFI—I'd wanted a full-black outfit. I tried to explain this but the words didn't come out right. The girl looked embarrassed and they went away.

When I think about that boy and girl now—and I do, in regular, fleeting snatches, a few times a year—I realize it's obvious that far from alternative outsiders (or whatever you want to call it), they were so beautifully and visibly normal, LiveJournal Millennial fairy-story, *straight*, in a way I've never been and am still waiting to be.

Ten years later, drugged and bleeding from my new vagina, returned to my childhood scenes of dark and clanking old Winnipeg walk-ups, the persistence of those two lingering lovers on my dreams comes into sharper focus when I think about all the boys I've chased and fucked since I transitioned. A lot of them were jerks, but the pairing of their bodies with mine felt so giddily and rushingly—*correct*. But in a frenzied and chemical way, correct like drugs feel correct, momentary brain-cleansers that let me feel like a regular girl—that let me forget that I was trans. (Large. Mannish. Sadly ugly. "Why not? *This* is why not.") And part and parcel: all these movies and songs about boys and girls suddenly, for once, felt like they applied. The culture of romance—even when I thought I was a hetero dude myself—never fit even marginally right, until I wanted a man to touch my hair and lift my cheek toward his lips. A girl and a boy cuddle-walking down the sidewalk. There's this AFI song called "The Days of the Phoenix."

I still like dudes, but I'd like to think now I know the score a little better. And I've got my troubles, but a lack of love isn't among them. Neither, still, is the abundance of good memories from my past, which I don't want my adult exasperation and roughed-up faith in my hometown to dilute. I don't.

With my family's reinvention, and then my own, it feels pretty juvenile and uninsightful to still think about being normal (a term our new land was supposed to rue). Yet, I would still gladly vanish it all and restart as the girl with the eyeliner and the boy with the devilock, cuddle-walking around and around the high school on an uncommonly sunny winter day in the Pacific Northwest. Part of me even believes the two of them are still together. What fairytale thoughts, eh?

Garrison Keillor once came and performed in Eugene. At the Cuthbert, just over the Ferry Street Bridge. My mom and I went. He did his old-timey Midwestern show thing and made jokes like, "Ah yes, Eugene, Oregon, where even the Republicans recycle." The crowd loved it. When we left, there was a lineup of cars waiting to go south over the bridge, but we had a clear lane going north, on Coburg, back home.

It was my last night back visiting for the summer. I was going back to New York the next day and, when I did, I was starting hormones. When I'd told my mother this, she cried. Then she said, "Your acne will get better." Then her face turned mean and she said, "You're going to have to take better care of your toenails. They're gross. No woman would let their toenails look as bad as yours." I said, "I know, I'm sorry, you're right, yes." And she said, "I'm serious. No woman would let that happen." And though I indeed felt gross (and ugly, and wretched, and selfish), there was one emotion I felt over all of it: lucky. Lucky to be there, lucky she was speaking to me, lucky to grow up in this town, lucky to hear what no woman would do, lucky to be allowed to exist at all.

Trish Bendix

Erasure

My name is missing. It's missing on purpose. The person who penned this obituary decided to exclude my existence.

Two of my wife's family members died recently: her 108-year-old great-grandmother, and her grandfather, both on her maternal side. Their obituaries ran a month apart in the same small-town, Midwestern paper, both listing many survivors, a testament to their strong genes. Beside everyone's names were their spouses, all except for "Julie." Julie had none.

"They didn't list you," Julie said before I had the chance to see for myself. "I think my mom wrote it."

I looked for myself, reading the tribute to her great-grandmother.

I don't know if I thought she'd missed it somehow, but I needed to see the omission for myself. "But what about your grandpa's?"

She shook her head, sad, and at first I thought she was embarrassed, like she'd done something shameful. Then I could see it was anger.

"I'm going to say something about it. He was at our wedding. He liked you."

I thought back to our wedding, two years ago this month. Her grandpa had touched my arm and said something softly that I couldn't understand. The music was too loud, his voice too hard to hear. I asked him to repeat himself and it was still unintelligible. "I wish I knew what he'd said," I told Julie. "I'm sure he was saying you looked beautiful," she said. "He was always saying really nice things to women."

Her grandpa had stood and watched with everyone else in the family (save for one religious grandmother on the other side) as Julie and I exchanged rings and vows, and signed our legal marriage certificate in the state of Iowa. He'd been there to celebrate with us, and now in his passing, that was erased. The writer of his obituary had made a conscious decision to pretend it hadn't happened, that one of the happiest days of my life didn't count.

The person who penned this final salute to a member of their family can come to my wedding. They can look me in the eye at gatherings, they can send me birthday cards and holiday wishes. But I'm never part of the family. Not if it means they have to put my name next to their daughter's in a public forum. Not if the neighbors might see.

When she came back from the funeral, I asked if Julie if she'd said anything.

"No, not yet. It wasn't the right time."

I couldn't blame her. She spent the few days she had with her family grieving over two family members, and also her grandma's recent cancer diagnosis. There were a lot of emotions and memories and things to discuss. It wasn't the top priority. It didn't have to be.

I wonder if the writer of the obituary agonized over their decision at all. Did they think, "What should I do? Should I include the name of Julie's wife?" Maybe they don't truly see me as "Julie's wife." Maybe they thought our wedding was a big song-and-dance that they became spectators of to be courteous, but lost that feeling of graciousness or niceties when it comes to publicizing their family and anyone who cares to read every single name written under "survivors" in a single person's newspaper farewell. Did they think, "I wonder if Julie will notice?" Did they think, "I wonder if Julie will care?" Did they assume yes, she might do both of those things and yet, what someone else in town thinks about seeing two women's names together might notice and care is of more importance? Maybe they think God reads the newspaper but casts a blind eye toward gay weddings.

It's a situation like this that keeps me grounded in reality. What does it take to earn love and respect from someone who says they have it for you but just can't show it? When will I deserve to have my name alongside Julie's like her brother has his wife's and his children's? I can come out over and over again but I am still kept closeted. I'm silenced, I'm erased. I don't exist.

Maybe what he'd said to me was a warning. "Don't get too far ahead of yourself. The world's not with you yet."

Chelsia A. Rice

We're Not Going Anywhere

Mostly I sense her, but sometimes I see her in the haze of half-opened eyes, the pain manifesting as pressure, the painkillers surging under the pulse of my thumb, which comes to life at the same time as every other sensation in my body: tingling, throbbing, burning, aching, swelling.

She is there on the cot beside me, or she is there gently blotting away the leftover rust of iodine and blood that has pooled in the creases around my thighs and in my navel. It's evening, and we're just beyond an eight-hour open surgery at Mayo Clinic. I feel movement when she comes near. She takes a cool, wet hand towel and dabs my head when I am flushed. She will walk next to me when I take my first couple of steps from the bed and quickly seat myself in a chair, while I hang onto the cart and walk down the hall, looking like an old man who steadies himself on a cane. Later, she will wash me while I sit on a retractable metal seat in the mauve-tiled bathroom, holding the tubes that are protruding from my body: a stent on one side and a drain on the other, an indwelling catheter strapped to my leg, fluids hydrating my body through a port in my chest, and an IV inserted into my arm. She will spend five days watching over me while I recover in the hospital bed with machines attached to all of my limbs, buzzing, beeping, and alarming every hour of our stay. I am a woman she barely recognizes: bald and emaciated, torn apart and sewn back together. She does not remember our past, nor does she believe that there will be a future; because there is only right now, and because she's "not going anywhere," just as she said in the months after we first met over a decade ago.

Way back when, in 2004, it was the glint of her jade gauged earring and the slope of her neck that caught my attention. She was listening to the volley of arguments for and against gay marriage, and I was sitting in a row of seats behind her. It was just before the election, and an amendment was being voted on to amend the Oregon Constitution, my state's constitution, the state where I'd lived and grown up. Measure 36 would define marriage as a union between one man and one woman. I'd organized the panel at the community college that I was attending and was actively fighting the measure, not because I had marriage in mind for myself, but because my mothers could never get legally married when I was a child and had settled instead for a unity ceremony. I didn't imagine that someday I'd be with a woman I'd want to marry. I already knew, because of my parents' sixteen-year relationship, all of the important legal benefits that could be secured for a committed couple with a state-recognized marriage. I had no need for them at that point, but it wouldn't be long before I did.

The first time she asked me to marry her it was just a few weeks after I had moved in. On a January night we were walking home

from the bus stop after some drinks with friends. It was cold and
wet, a typical winter day in Portland, and everything was soaked.
Outside of her apartment, just before we walked in, she dropped
to her knees on the sidewalk and asked me. I said yes. Then there
was the time she walked urgently out of the kitchen where she
was making dinner and crouched before me at the couch where
I sat and asked again, "Someday, will you marry me?" I said yes
again. And there were many rings to demonstrate our commitment, none of them worth much. There was the orange one
made of stone that I broke by simply slapping my hand on a table
during a lunchtime outburst of laughter. There was a silver band
with unfurling vines that encircled a red gemstone in the shape
of a teardrop. Then there was a green emerald centered in a bulky
silver band that watched me as an eye would. That one was my
favorite because it was like my own eye looking back at me, as
green as mine, telling me every day that she was the one, that I
only needed to place myself in the center of it. It would be six
years from the day I moved in that first time, nearly to the day,
that she'd ask me to marry her for the third time.

    During winter break, in my last year of graduate school, I took
her to the library and into the literary magazine stacks—my favorite place to study. I stooped to run my fingers along the small
and delicate spines of books in which I hoped to someday appear.
When I came up she had placed a small box on the top of the
shelf between us. With her eyebrows arched high and an uncertain look on her face, she said, "Will you be with me until you
can't stand me anymore?" She didn't say the M-word, but I knew
what she meant, and her question was severe, a commitment that
neither of us would take lightly. There was a fleeting moment of
silence after she asked. I said yes again, but we didn't jump up and
down in celebration. As we set off for home just a few moments
later with the simple silver band around my finger, we returned to
my under-weatherized rental house where I lived for the duration

of graduate school. We cooked a meal and lay on the couch together holding one another, wondering what might come for us going forward, despite the national conversation, which was just beginning to murmur the words "marriage for all" state by state.

Graduate school ended and I moved to Helena, Montana, to join her. In the spring of 2012, she is teaching history to dropouts, and I am teaching college writing as an adjunct while working part-time for an estate planning attorney. In the law office I answer phones and emails, greet clients when they arrive, and offer them coffee or water. I write letters and draw up documents, act as a witness for signings, and make copies for files. To better understand the estate planning process my boss encourages my partner and me to draw up our own estate plan, and he'll do it pro bono as part of the training. The week before we set off for our Oregon trip, we draw up our powers of attorney and health care powers of attorney. He says we don't want to travel without them.

So we fold and slide them into a manila envelope and put them in our glove box before we drive across the western US toward southern Oregon, where we'll attend my family reunion. Along the way I keep imagining what I'll have to do to get to our documents if we are in a head-on crash and I go through the windshield. Will I be able to crawl back to the car and get them before they drag us away from the scene in separate ambulances? I imagine myself coming to on the side of the road and realizing that I don't have the ability to get the documents. I imagine the entire car going up in flames before I can reach them.

It's on the trip across central Oregon that we get a text message from a friend back home that reads, "The school board has voted to allow partner benefits beginning in fall!" We are driving along the Oregon Trail at that exact moment, and as we pass by the stone markers that stand along the highway, I am reminded of pioneers who persisted despite unforgiving landscape. Back in Montana there are no civil unions, no domestic partnerships, no gay marriages. This small concession is a token of equality that twelve strangers gave to us, and though it's not enough, it's something.

A few days later, at our campsite along the Rogue River, I notice the burn for the first time. At a rest area heading south, I see the first few drops of blood appear in the toilet. At first I convince myself that I'm spotting, even though I track my periods, and I'm just on the other side of one. Then I convince myself that I have a bladder infection, a really bad one, and perhaps I'm just not clean enough from our camping excursion despite nightly scrubbing up under a solar shower. When we reach my family, we have three days of hot showers and indoor plumbing. The burning lasts long after I urinate, and I can now see the blood dissipate on the floor of the shower stall.

It's cancer. I sense this even before there are images to prove it, when I first see the drops of blood in the toilet, and so does she, though she does not say it.

It's not until I get home, a week later, that I drop in to see a nurse for a urinalysis. Every second of that visit is filled with regret. I remember every moment, from arriving in the waiting room to peeing into the cup, from waiting for the results to the nurse's instruction afterward. I already knew I was making a mistake going to see a doctor for the symptoms. I knew I was setting myself up to be denied for a preexisting condition. I had heard the stories and had watched the documentaries. I wanted to play by the rules, but I couldn't.

If it doesn't go away, the nurse says, give us a call.

It doesn't go away. I see a gynecologist who tells me, "This isn't my department. You should make an appointment with a urologist."

It's cancer, but the urologist tells me to wait until I have insurance to get a more thorough exam. *It's cancer*, but the tumor continues growing inside of me, and the color of my urine darkens to rust.

When my partner calls the school district to inquire about the benefits, we are told that the school board got the cart before the horse. "We don't even have a form created yet," said the woman on the end of the line. According to her, "the nine of [us] will have to wait while the other fourteen hundred people that are in the system are processed." We write a letter to the superintendent about her discriminatory remarks. We never get a response.

After we finally get the rundown of what we need to get coverage, we show up at the benefits office with six of the thirteen kinds of acceptable documents that are necessary to prove that my partner and I are in a committed relationship. We've just left the law office where I work part time, and we've finally completed our estate plan. We give the benefits manager a copy of our wills, living wills, powers of attorney, health care powers of attorney, proof of our joint checking account, which has been in place for over six months, and our rental contract. Our documents are carefully examined, dates are scrutinized, and copies are made. Coverage will begin October 1. I get home and call the urologist to schedule an appointment for an exam and a CT scan for the third. This is what I was told to do: Go get insurance and come back when you are covered. By then I'd been burning and bleeding since July. What were a few more weeks to see a doctor?

It's cancer is what I know when I see the black bulge on my bladder but don't hear from the doctor because my ears are ringing as she points to it. The overhead fluorescents are bleaching out everything except for the black and white image of my internal organs, and all I can feel is a cry of terror crawling out from inside of me. I swallow it down and focus on the steady hand of my partner holding my leg.

After the first surgery, a biopsy, we learned the bladder cancer was a rare kind, one that is only two percent of the cases that are diagnosed in the US. The doctors in Montana said they had never seen this kind of cancer before, and they weren't certain what to do to treat it. They send us to another state, to a tertiary institution, to Mayo Clinic in the heartland of the nation. It's another place where two adults who've committed their lives to one another aren't equal, where we have to make sure to file our documents proving our relationship so she may speak for me when I am unable, and so they can tell her what is going on when I have been silenced by surgery. We go to Mayo and check in with our documents in hand. It is the first order of business when we arrive.

When I begin chemo the insurance company turns me down for a preexisting condition just as I expected. Then we learn we are being taxed an extra $250 a month because we are not married, but we can't get married in the state in which we live. In the hours between treatments, I exhaust myself by writing letters and making phone calls to providers and insurance companies. I try to make sense of the legal jargon despite my inability to think clearly. I learn we have to remain insured in order to get services at Mayo, and that we have to continue paying for insurance that refuses to cover me. My love works an eight-hour day and comes home to make dinner for me because I cannot stand for long over a hot stove, or risk cutting my finger with a knife for fear that infection will overtake my body faster than the cancer. She comes home and reminds me to get up to go to the bathroom, then steadies my clumsy and feeble body as we walk to it on the other side of the house. She returns me to the dark bedroom where the curtains are always drawn, and I sleep for three days straight. She feeds me scrambled eggs with a spoon while I lay still in the dark chemocoma that has overtaken me.

I am nauseated, numb, tingling, in pain. My brain is steeped in chemicals, my speech affected, my eyes blurred, my skin raw, my mouth and nose full of sores. And I'm so cold, yet so hot, and I have to somehow stay on the phone, stay on the insurance company, stay up to date on my applications for financial assistance because my life depends on getting that surgery at the end of chemotherapy, and I can't get surgery without insurance or a $20,000 down payment.

We spend that year of our life proving our relationship to hospitals and insurance company representatives, making appeals to strangers who sit around tables and determine who can access certain services and who is actually considered family. Strangers in communities across the nation, people who've never been in a relationship like mine, are voting on whether or not our relationship counts, or if we can be married. People on television discuss our relationship in terms of whether or not it is worthy of recognition; decisions are made about a relationship in which they have never been and can never see inside.

And my love, she stands by me as I deteriorate, she makes me food, and she makes me giggle. She doesn't stop doing the things we love to do because she knows it may be the last time we ever do them.

I arrived for surgery on May 1, at 5:00 a.m. and didn't believe I would ever come out. The last thing I saw was the ceiling of the operating room and the nurses approaching. I didn't understand how a body could be opened so wide for so long. They take out my bladder, my ovaries, fallopian tubes, uterus, cervix, and forty-six lymph nodes. They take out eighteen inches of my bowel and create a reservoir that they put back inside me. They reconnect all the necessary parts and sew me back together. In the waiting room she watched a monitor and waited for eight hours with my father, his wife, and our best friend. I was listed as a number, my progress tracked from admittance to completion. They came at the end of the day and told her that everything went well, that it didn't take as long as they expected, that they'd know the results of the pathology in a few days.

Four days after my surgery the doctor said, "I think we can call this a win." I rested my chin on her shoulder when she gently wrapped her arms around me in my hospital bed. Fourteen days after my surgery we learn that Minnesota is the twelfth state in the nation to allow gay marriage. On that day, we have our binoculars pointed out into the backyard of the apartment we are renting while I recover in Rochester. We are watching colorful ribbons lace through the trees. Spring has arrived and the warblers are migrating.

On the one-year anniversary of my diagnosis, we marry in Washington while we are in Seattle for a weekend retreat to celebrate our birthdays. We have endured a long-distance relationship and graduate school, we have faced cancer, and we know we will face so much more. On the only sunny day of that weekend, a Saturday, outside of the city hall, with the eyes of just a few to witness us, we turn to each other and vow. Our commitment is one we made so long ago, one we knew we'd make from the very start, and I think I can speak for us both when I say, though we already knew our relationship would endure whatever we might face, there was a moment in the tangerine glow of fall leaves warming our faces that we realized the ceremony was so much more than paperwork.

Today I am cancer-free. Like most nights, tonight I sit at the edge of our bed with each of my legs wrapped from toe to groin with six compression bandages. I complain that I feel like a mutant since my legs are swollen to twice their normal size and jiggle from the accumulation of fluid that only these bandages can disperse. With the removal of my lymph nodes has come lymphedema, a chronic condition for which there is no cure. I take my wedding ring off before my fingers begin to swell and set it on the nightstand. My joints swell with arthritis, something the chemo left behind in its wake. I quickly shimmy under the sheets and smile. "Don't look!" I say, giggling as I do every night, hiding myself beneath the covers no matter how futile the act. I am quite self-conscious about my body, but I have to joke about it. There's no hiding what's become of me, and there's no ignoring the fact that I have to wear this damn absorbent underwear to bed because my new bladder, the one the doctors had to create out of my bowel in order for me to live a somewhat normal life, doesn't hold urine through the night. I roll clumsily onto my side, my bandaged legs round and awkwardly pitched atop one another, and she turns onto her side to meet my gaze.

I sigh. "Does seeing me like this bother you?"

"It's our new normal," she says. "I don't even see it anymore."

I know she sees all of it, perhaps more clearly than I, but it is at this moment that it all comes together. She's not going anywhere, and neither am I.

Ryka Aoki

Sakura, Ayame, and a Cotton Judogi

One day, should the dreams of my dreams come true, I would love to be married while wearing a kimono. In my eyes, kimono are some of the most beautiful garments created. Kimono take my breath away; their colors and patterns bring songs and poetry, fireflies and wind. I was born in the springtime, so perhaps it's fate that I should dream of sleeves swept with silent, gentle sakura or footsteps wrapped in stylized purple sweeps of ayame.

But for now, I spend far more time wearing another archetypal Japanese garment: my judogi. White cotton, double-woven, heavy, much of the judogi's beauty comes from its unswerving dedication to be what it has to be. My current gi has had the chance to soften over the years, though the seams still leave crosshatched cuts and bruises where a student has gripped my arm with a little too much raw strength.

Since I no longer compete, the gi I wear today has lasted far longer than its predecessors, whose ripped and bloodstained shreds I sometimes show my students when I reflect upon my past training. It's a far more effective display of tenacity than a mere black belt, no matter how many embroidered stripes it might display.

Looking back upon nearly four decades of judo, I am proud of what I have done, and how far I have come. I honed my judo in an exquisitely functional, but often vicious place whose unswerving mission was winning. Although surviving that dojo helped make me strong, even a champion, I would not want my current students to learn in an environment so mercilessly focused upon fighting.

My current students are queer youth, sometimes kicked out of the house, abused, at risk. For the past three years, I've taught self-defense to LGBTQ youth at the Los Angeles Gay and Lesbian Center. One student sits on the side of the mat with a broken arm. Two months ago he was jumped in his neighborhood and the bone still hasn't knit. Some of my students have been abused so badly, they can't even form a fist without crying. Some of them can't even be touched; others move like awkward puppets, as if needing safe distance from their bodies.

At my old dojo, my current students would have been targeted, hunted, thought of as hopeless or stupid…that is, if they were thought of at all.

Protect the weak. Behave honorably. Respect humanity. Statements like these are proudly displayed in nearly every martial arts studio or dojo. But tell an instructor you're gay and homeless. You're HIV+. You have PTSD, and still wet your bed. Try being young, queer, and homeless, and you may perceive a rift between the streets of Los Angeles and heroic brushstrokes on a rice paper scroll.

Hopeless. Stupid.
Trauma can do that to you.

When strident, loving queers talk of marriage equality, and family, and the bonds of everlasting love, it reminds me that I have yet to understand a love that does not cost, or hurt—but can protect and shelter. What for others is simply a *given*—for me, has been *taken*.

Just as I would never judge my old senseis, I understand that for some, this debate, and this fight around it, is integral to who they are, perhaps even part of why they were put on this earth. Yet, just as so much focus on fighting leaves out those who would never fight, having marriage as a goal excludes those of us who are now quite simply too battered, too wounded, too broken to bear.

Rallying around LGBTQ marriage presumes a world where queer and LGBTQ interests have intersected to a point where queers are just like everyone else, ready to love whomever they want and enter a domestic life with parent-teacher conferences, a backyard garden with a persimmon tree, perhaps a kitchen with a breakfast nook and granite countertops.

Meanwhile, I can't even keep a dog without worrying if someone might kill it. When it comes to marriage, I am still not even sure of the right questions to ask. How does one become ready for marriage, or even know where to start? What safeguards are in place? Do I put the police on speed dial? What about when my spouse gets mad and starts throwing things? What if my phone dies? Do I have a set of keys to my best friend's apartment? Can I get to my car?

For me, the belief that marriage is the next step in LGBTQ activism underlines a difference between what the LGBTQ community desires and what the queer community is able to give. It seems to presume that somehow this terrified, queer Asian trans girl should have held enough of herself together, not only to be somewhat functional, but on her way to being ready to fight for the right to take a wife, become a mother, consider children.

Yet why would I want to bind myself within a relationship when I know what happens to me whenever I fall in love?

Sometimes I would rather bury what I have felt and seen, but it is important to remember that abuse is an unavoidable part of queer community. As my students, friends, and nightmares remind me. As each memorial, email, or terrifying Facebook notification makes it impossible to forget. Whether from parents, or lovers, or friends, or all of the above, people are beaten and kicked out because they are queer.

Queer people die because they are queer. And beyond the proud and powerful coming-out narratives, there are secrets still in the closet, not by choice, nor for lack of effort, but because they have been pressed in the walls, leached through the paint, burned into the plaster and two-by-fours beneath. This is where safe words aren't used, where terror happens and all hell's playground utters not a single, unsmothered sound.

The fight for marriage equality asks from me a perception that I neither share nor comprehend. Why would I ever want to create a place like my childhood bedroom? Why would I ever want to go back where something pure and pretty was lost? It's not how or even if I should get married, but *why?*

The most terrible lesson of abuse, provided you've survived, is knowing that any love you have can be turned against you, that any trust can be broken like a father breaks his word. That all the hopes of true love mean nothing when you've breathed the wrong way, or said too much, or the person gets mad for some reason you completely don't understand. Anything you have can be taken away; your toys can be thrown, or used to whip you; your favorite stuffed animal can be held over your face while you struggle and claw into the night.

Which is most likely why my mother once said that I would be lucky to find anyone who could ever put up with me.

Have you ever been at a café in midmorning when the young moms gather with their mom bags and mom hair and mom strollers with their mom babies to talk mom things? It is a supportive, lively, engaged discussion, but when you're not at a place for it, you cringe at even the most well-meaning, "I'm sure one day you'll be a mom, too." Even the gentlest smiles, and reassurances that "the right time will come" assume that either I have fallen short, been unlucky, not met the right guy, or spent too much time on my career.

I know that my experiences have damaged me, have injured me, but even those trying to be helpful, to be gentle, do not help when they assume that marriage is my goal. How to get married, the right to get married, when are you going to finally get married...Such discussions not only prescribe a timetable for my recovery: they prioritize my life, dictate a pathway to a certain view of liberation, recovery, and health.

I will forever resist such talk. Not merely for me, but for others I know who are not ready, not able, or even not interested in setting marriage as a milestone in their lives. Within each refuge there should be refuge. Within any community of wounded, there should be equal acceptance for those who heal quickly, those who heal slowly, and those who have forgotten what it is to fall asleep in another's arms.

For some, marriage seems to be obvious. That one could have a relationship without violence or yelling is as natural as planting a field in spring and coming for harvest in the fall. It's not that they don't need to work at it; of course they do. It's just for them, marriage is as realistic as what germinates from the soil, a natural outcome of sun, and seasons, and seed.

Yet there is so much more to marriage than marriage. Marriage is also who is left behind, not through what has been legislated, but what has been scarred. Even when the LGBTQ mother ship rises toward its goal of total marriage equality, there will still be everyone who is unwilling, unable, or who have created different ways to express love or commitment or trust. And they will still be queer.

In my childhood home, I heard I was not loved as much as my sister. I was hit, and bruised, kept home from school, and told not to whisper a word. I was told I could be killed in my own bed when I fell asleep. For me, this is what parents do. And, as my template for what is done in the name of love, I have taken this forward, possibly poisoning every relationship I have ever had.

I laugh when people call me marrying material; I have been in relationships almost constantly from the time I was eighteen. I have been called sweet, nice, even romantic. And at times, I might be. At least it feels like it. And when they say it, I melt inside, I blush, I want to find out what tea they like, their favorite soap. I want to cook the dishes of their childhoods. Anything to make them happy as long as possible, before the hell inevitably begins.

I do try to be happy for those who have found themselves with others, and I even now am trying to make a relationship work with someone I love—but in my head is this terrible certainty that love turns ugly when the door is finally locked. Friends say otherwise, therapists say otherwise, common sense and every poem I ever write says otherwise.

But for now, I live in a world where nothing is safe, where I shouldn't trust honesty, or beauty, but I hunger for them anyway, like an addict might, knowing all the promises of forever haven't lasted worth a damn. Where I can read another lover, know what she wants to hear, and how to get a smile. Where an "I love you" buys another night I've kept the pain at bay.

Sometimes I get so frustrated. Who decided that queer marriage would make it all better? "Being free to love whom you choose" is a great slogan, but so much cruelty has been buried, locked behind closed doors, under such public declaration of love!

Who decides that queers should fight to be married or to be let into the army? Of course each is an important, even critical issue—but who decides what is to be the issue? What next? The priesthood? The NFL?

Besides, why should queer identity depend upon such battles? I yearn for a queer identity that is—well—queer. Rather than argue over what one is, I wish for a queerness that rests upon what one is not. I yearn for a queer identity whose existence affirms that even outside definitions and institutions, human beings can still exist, find safety, and even thrive.

I look forward to a day when being queer is enough to be queer. When we don't need an issue around which to rally. I wish for a love or identity or a life that does not need an issue of the day to be meaningful or to belong. I look forward to a time when the scars one feels match the scars one cares to see. Where we can talk of loud noises and nightmares, and broken glass and cold sweats and even those quiet wishes that one might disappear into having never been alive.

I am not saying that I find the marriage or the motherhood questions or any of their related struggles unworthy of action and financing and passion and courage. I would love a world with marriage equality. I look forward to one day being able to keep a dog. Where I tell myself I might get married. Where I might have a child. Where my experience as a child abuse survivor might help me become a better partner and parent. Where I might even ride a motorcycle.

And though my life is not poetry, I wish it could be, with all my power as a writer or a dreamer, I wish I could write my past away as a metaphor, a plot device. I wish I could tell you how I crafted my scars to further a political cause, or bring our queer family closer together, or illustrate how even abuse can end philosophically, with wisdom and new gratitude for life.

I will dream of kimonos with sakura, and ayame, with flowing sleeves that swish with the sound of rain. And I will do my best to lie next to my love in the middle of the night, even as I tremble, to lose myself in the first time we kissed, the first roller coaster we ever rode, on that magical summer afternoon.

I will dream of feeling right enough, innocent enough to wear a silken wedding kimono. To be safe enough to bow, smile, share a single cup of rice wine with all the hope, wonder, and poetry that I have ever held sacred and dear.

However, I will also work with all my being for a world with better health care, safer shelters for queer youth, more ways to combat bullying. And for now, rather than fight for marriage, I would rather devote my time to nurture my students, to help them realize that self-defense starts with loving the selves they are defending.

And more than trying to love the right partner, I'm trying to love the me that belongs to me, not merely give away, but to have and hold, perhaps for the first time in my life.

So for now, I will pull my hair into a ponytail, put on my judogi and my best smile, and greet my students. I'll listen to them speak and breathe, watch them move and sit still. I will work to help them discover that their bodies are far more than what they might have thought. As they make friends, practice, learn, and laugh, there will be so much shared beauty, pride, and strength.

And maybe a few tears. But it's okay.

There will always be time for tears.

Tucker Garcia

The Boys' Club

As I looked down over the forty-eight acres of hilly fields it was
my responsibility to maintain, it was hard not to be daunted by
the task at hand. A midsummer heat wave lay like a heavy blanket
over the lush hills of western Massachusetts. It was just before
noon and already the humidity and heat had sapped my body
of energy. I stuck my pitchfork into the earth and removed my
hat to wipe the sweat from my forehead with my already damp
T-shirt. Cleaning the horse refuse out of the pastures was a dawn-
to-dusk task on the best of days, and this was certainly not one
of those.

The inside of my mouth felt woolly, so I grabbed my water
bottle from the large, bright orange bucket loader I had parked
nearby. It was made for heavy lifting, but even with its use the
going was slow. It had taken me most of the morning to fill the
bucket only twice and dump the loads into the manure pile a

quarter mile down the winding driveway. I estimated that I had at least three more loads in this pasture alone.

"And just two more pastures to go…" I sighed and drained the contents of the water bottle. I decided it was as good a time as any to march back up to the house for a refill. The pastures were all enclosed by an electric fence that was meant to keep the horses in check, and they respected it. I, on the other hand, thinking myself superior to horse and fence alike, attempted to slip under the lowest rope. I received a good zap on my back, but neither this shock nor the many before it would be enough to prevent the dozens more I would experience that summer.

My boss's house stood at the top of the hill. It was a large structure, simple enough in its construction. A balcony-style porch wrapped around two of its sides and connected to a stone patio that was littered with lawn furniture and décor from a party that had taken place early in the season. The house's once-gray finish had been stripped away by a crew of three painters who were now starting to apply the first of several coats of new color. I often saw them scrambling up and down ladders, white pants spattered with paint, cigarettes dangling from their mouths, and shirts hanging from their back pockets like flags of their masculinity. As I approached I heard them yelling, which seemed to be their primary form of communication.

Johnny, the oldest of the crew, had skin so sunbaked it resembled the callused palms of my hands. White-gray hair wisped out from under his ball cap, and a small belly hung over his not-so-tightly fastened belt. He was yelling at Zack, one of the younger painters, who had tried to mount the ladder to the roof before Johnny had gotten off of it. Zack had small, dark eyes that darted from place to place but never seemed to settle on anything. He didn't have much to say, but chortled along at Johnny's jokes like a loyal pet. His teeth were yellowed and broken from years of cigarettes and alcohol abuse. Various fading tattoos decorated his sun-leathered skin. There was a dream catcher on his chest; its feathers dangled down to his stomach. An Asian-style dragon sprawled across his back, mouth wide and claws grasping. Crop circles spiraled out into tiny dots on his shoulders, and tribal bands twisted down his arms.

"Watch out, you little tailgunner!" Johnny said. "Don't be coming after my ass like that."

My teeth clenched tight, forming a cage to keep my eager tongue in check as Zack held up his hands and gave a laugh. They had been taunting one another with gay and sexist jokes all summer, only stopping in the presence of our boss's wife.

I walked past the ladders and into the garage to refill my water bottle. The shade of the building was an instant relief, so I sat for a moment on an upturned bucket and stretched my shoulders and back. My muscles groaned and my spine creaked, but try as I might I could get no relief; my movement was too limited by the clothing that kept my secrets.

"Maggie!" Johnny's voice came booming down from above. "Oh whiny little Maggie!"

"Maggie's not here right now," said Mikey, the third and youngest painter, appearing from around the corner with his middle finger erected in Johnny's general direction.

"Oh what's the matter, sweetheart?" Johnny taunted as he came down the ladder.

"You give me the gayest jobs." Mikey had already adopted the whine that had won him the nickname.

"That's because I give you jobs you can handle, Maggie." Johnny's face split into a yellow-toothed grin as he flipped his paintbrush around and slapped its handle into Mikey's palm. "Now go wash my paintbrush, sugar."

Mikey's whine continued on under his breath as he walked to the sink to do as he was told. Johnny lit a cigarette, looked my way and gave me a nod. I nodded back, jaw clenched and eyes narrowed, trying to look more like the "man's man" I knew I wasn't.

"Hey, did you bring lunch again today or do you wanna come down to town with us and grab some food?" he said on an exhale, leaning against the doorframe.

"Yeah, I do need food actually." My mouth produced the words of its own accord, as it so often does, and a split second later my brain caught up. Not only had I brought a lunch from home that day, I was actually afraid of being alone with these men away from the safety of the house. Every off-color remark that had left me nervous echoed in my head. My skin crawled at the memory of shrinking into myself under their gaze, so certain that the vague contours of my body would give me away. But despite this terror, I was exhilarated. I realized with a rush why they had never stopped short when cracking jokes in my presence in the same way that they had around the boss's wife. They had never expected the comments to bother me, had no idea that underneath my mud-stained shirt were breasts pressed flat by a corset-tight compression tank. I was invisible among them, something that I had waited my entire life to achieve. This was it. This was what it felt like to be in the boys' club.

"Cool. There's room in the truck if you wanna ride along with us." He emitted a steady stream of smoke with his words, and my already-limited breaths became shorter. My lungs immediately vetoed the idea of sitting in a truck with three chimneys as we made our way to town, and my brain quickly agreed that taking my own car would be safer. In case my mouth decided to act of its own accord again, every awful scenario involving the many miles of rural back road between the house and the restaurant flashed through my mind in rapid succession. It seemed unlikely that the painters had hatched any sinister plans, but this hyper-awareness of safety had become a normal part of my everyday existence.

"I'll just meet you there. I gotta get gas anyways," I lied again. I had just topped off my car and filled eight cans for the farm equipment the day before. I held my breath and hoped he wouldn't mention that fact.

"Alright. Well, we're probably gonna go in around five or so, once these ladies get their acts together." He gestured with his cigarette to Zack and Mikey, who were now fighting over sink space. As I stood, Johnny pulled his shirt from his back pocket, struggled to put it on over his cap, and eventually succeeded. Stained with paint of all colors, the T-shirt's orange Hooters' logo still stood out proudly across his chest.

The air conditioning in my blue Ford hatchback was broken and the day was so hot that the breeze from the windows provided no relief. I rolled in to the center of town, which consisted of three equally shabby buildings, all on the right-hand side of the road, all within a few hundred feet of one another. The first held a pharmacy and hardware store. The second building was a gas station. The final lot was home to a small liquor store and pizza parlor. I pulled in and entered the restaurant. The frigid blast of air conditioning made my skin prickle and constrict. Inside there were only seven booths, the red vinyl upholstery on each of them worn and cracking. Mismatched amateur paintings hung along the walls and a tower of pizza boxes was stacked to the dusty ceiling in the back corner.

A college-aged girl behind the counter was ringing up an older gentleman and paused to tell me to seat myself. The paper place mats on the tables were littered with advertisements from local businesses. I studied the low-budget graphic designs and cheesy slogans while I waited. About ten minutes had passed when the door opened again.

"Hey boys!" the waitress called out.

"Hey there, darlin'!" Johnny's voice boomed back and I turned to wave and catch their attention. Johnny and Zack slid into the booth opposite me and Mikey parked himself by my side. Having ignored me since I arrived, the waitress now hustled over quickly once the painters had settled, bringing silverware but no menus.

"What can I get for you guys today?" She turned to Mikey first, beaming down at him.

"Turkey sub with fries. Dr. Pepper," he said not looking back at her.

"Mmk. And for you, hun?" She turned to Johnny.

"I'm trying to be healthier, so I'm gonna get the grilled chicken wrap, no fries and a Diet Coke. Thanks, sweetheart."

"And..." Zack began, as the waitress looked his way.

"He's really in the mood for some tossed salad," Johnny interrupted with a wink and a laugh.

"Oh, stop it!" The waitress laughed along, but her smile died on her dimpled cheeks and never made it to her eyes.

"I'm gonna get the cheeseburger sub, actually. And can I have onion rings and a Dr. Pepper?" The waitress nodded at Zack and turned to me. I was still unprepared, having not seen a menu, and in my panic ordered one of the three things I knew were available.

"I'll have a turkey sub, please." I smiled at her. Her heavily made-up eyes peered expectantly back at me.

"Lettuce, tomato, mayo?" she asked after an awkward pause.

"Yes please."

"Fries or onion rings?"

"Fries, please." I suddenly felt that I was being too polite and would somehow give myself away. None of the other men had bothered with manners. Would they realize I had been raised with a different set of expectations?

"And anything to drink?"

"Could I have a root beer?"

"Mmk. I'll put that right in for you guys and be back with your drinks in a bit." As she walked away, Johnny leaned out of the booth to watch her go.

"Maggie, why would you be banging that itty-bitty when you

could have a girl like that? Now *she's* got a great personality."
Johnny held his hands out in front of his chest to indicate breasts.
I cringed, the sixteen years of female socialization I had experienced begging me to come to her defense, to tell Johnny that she wasn't there for their viewing pleasure, to say anything that might shut him up and make him think. Instead, I began chewing the inside of my cheek, a sour taste at the back of my throat.

"Whatever." Mikey tapped away on his cell phone as his leg bounced up and down under the table in agitation. Before Johnny could mount a second attack, the waitress was back with our sodas.

"Your food will be done in a few." She set the drinks down in front of us, and Johnny leaned out of the booth once more as she walked away and let out a quiet whistle.

"And that can ain't bad either. I'm serious Maggie, you keep playing around with that itty-bitty and people are gonna to think you've got a problem with boobs. Maybe you're a tail gunner like this guy over here." He jerked his thumb in Zack's direction, releasing another laugh. Zack laughed along; having been with the same girlfriend for the better part of a decade, he knew his manhood wasn't really on trial. The taste in my mouth had gone from sour to acidic as my teeth clenched harder on my cheek.

"Screw off." Mikey's leg bounced faster.

"So sensitive. I think I'm striking a nerve here." Johnny jostled Zack playfully, nodding at Mikey. "Look Maggie, if you like to suck hose that's your business. I just don't want that shit around me."

"I'm not a faggot." Mikey's short fuse had reached its end just as a metallic rush flooded my mouth. He shouted, "You're a faggot!"

"Jeez-us. Calm down, Mikey. Don't make a damn scene."

Johnny looked around at the other two occupied booths, whose tenants seemed unaffected by Mikey's words. Johnny changed topics to the painting project and things quieted down.

When the waitress came back with our food, I found that choking back my words had left me with no appetite. I nibbled a few fries and had a bite or two of sandwich before asking for a to-go box. I excused myself, using the gas as reasoning for my early departure and left without waiting for my change. As I drove back toward the house I tongued the place where I had bit my cheek. At the restaurant blood flowed into my mouth in place of the words that I knew desperately needed to be said. The same words I had put down on paper and spoken in private so many times, promising myself I would use them to effect change. I wanted so badly to believe that I could make these men see the world differently, but my self-preservation instincts had kicked in. These men were old dogs with no desire to learn new tricks. They were comfortable in their boys' club, and I knew now that I didn't belong.

Fabian Romero

Allegiance to Scarcity
Marriage and Liberation

Mi abuela married at age thirteen, mi mama at seventeen, and I turned down my first proposal by the time I was fifteen.

At the time, I was a rosy-cheeked pocho girl returning to Mexico for a quick cultural immersion. By then the eight years of Americanization had changed me. The United States was at the center of my identity and my need to assimilate became the center of my existence—a way of surviving by blending in, and, in the process, pushing away my culture. I accepted the trope of the sexualized Latina and embraced it. In my CD player was a mix of Salsa music, the wrong kind of music for a Mexican kid from a pueblo with a mariachi and ranchera soundtrack. I no longer spoke in the same cadence. In my practice of centering English I had forgotten basic Spanish words. I no longer fit with the other muchachas en mi pueblo.

As the young man stood there waiting for my response about running away together to el norte and getting married, I went blank and shook. My whole body shook. I was trying so hard to make sense of my identity, and wasn't in a place of committing to any one idea, person, or place. A few things stopped me from getting married then. In the United States I had been exposed to a different life and different possibilities. Although some of those possibilities were about having more options for my future that would not be possible in my hometown because of socioeconomic factors, I also wanted to fit into American culture as much as possible. That meant lessening my ties to people who were not educated in the United States, who didn't speak English, and who were farmworkers.

More than anything, I believed early on that marriage needn't be the only way to be in this body and be loved, but I still didn't know the alternative.

At this time, at fifteen, I understood marriage as a duty, an unequal exchange. The gendered training that comes with centuries of colonization resulted in kitchen meetings where women were free to share frustrations. On both sides of the border this culture of chismeando—gossiping—in the safety of the kitchen was a part of my life. I listened. Abuse. Rape. Dependence. Fear. I can't recall the details and wouldn't want to reveal them if I could, but I heard about the reality of having no choice in survival for a woman or femme except by marriage. I understood it as survival; there was little choice, and it was often a tactic for breaking poverty—although that rarely ended in success. Even after marriages, most of my family still lives in extreme poverty. Often the women who had been married the longest were giving advice to newly married women to endure the violence, to accept the stresses from his alcoholism, to be strong.

I come from a small pueblo with a low rate of literacy, a high rate of extreme poverty, and few chances for education. Even at fifteen, I felt—but did not fully understand—the privileges afforded to me. These included literacy, education, fluency in English, and my high possibility of US citizenship. Most of the women in my family, especially those who came to the States in adulthood, don't have the same options as me.

What also complicated the idea of marriage for me was my gender. I was a tomboy for a lot of my life, but I also learned to perform gender well. I was an obedient child, a quality attributed to femininity, and learned to care for other people more than myself. Still, I spent years of my life trying to push the acceptable boundaries of femininity in my family and the limitations of gender with my clothes, my assertiveness, my confrontational personality, and with my priorities to excel in leadership-building school courses. I was a smart kid but I questioned authority often, spent most of my middle school years in detention, and failed classes that were meant for women. I failed a cooking class miserably. At home, I refused to learn to cook or take advice on how to be a good wife one day. Although I challenged gender, I was afraid that if I lived my life in my full gender expression and was true to my two-spirit identity, I would complicate things for myself unnecessarily.

I want to believe that I have always resisted marriage, but I think this understanding came gradually. As I decentered whiteness, as I decentered colonial thinking, as I became aware of oppression in my life, I began to make decisions and changes that centered my wholeness and complexities. But like many queer people of color, I survived by using drugs and alcohol until I became dependent on them. I know today that many queer people struggle with addiction, and that historically queer communities socialize in bar scenes. I remember when my casual drinking became daily drinking in my late teens. My relationship with drug abuse coincided with my relationship with my first boyfriend. We were together for seven years. In the last year of our relationship, he started talking about marriage seriously, and flashbacks of the kitchen advice rushed through me. I'd already seen the warning signs of future abuse: his put-downs hit deeper than punches. He had been what I needed in my life then, a way to find freedom. My very strict parents let me spend time out of the house with him, in hopes that I would come around and be like the other girls in la familia, but no matter how hard I tried, I couldn't. Before my twenty-first birthday, I broke up with him.

In my twenties, I found a community of queer people of color who were well-versed in power and privilege discourse, and who also supported and understood my identity. I found myself questioning marriage again. I had moved away from home, started dating women and gender-variant people. Since I was not under the rule of my traditional parents, I had the freedom to explore gender, discuss transitioning and the politics of being an androgynous female-assigned-at-birth person. I learned that my androgynous gender expression provides me with benefits from patriarchy. Masculine-appearing people are given legitimacy and validity. Learning this gave me a lens to challenge the abusive masculinity that I saw modeled in men and in marriage in my family. It was then that I made a commitment to break the cycle of abuse in my family—the same abuse I witnessed as a child and later heard about in the safety of kitchens—by embodying a decolonized masculinity. Men in my family carry on the legacies of colonizer violence, and control and ownership of women. Marriage has always felt like a site of repeating colonizer violence. Today I have the responsibility to reject that notion of ownership and dominance of femmes and women. In my body is the urgent desire to have loving relationships without fear of abuse. I feel the responsibility as a masculine, two-spirit person to change this, by changing myself and by helping others change too.

As I became aware of oppression and how people are excluded, I started to transform, and to feel the reality of privilege; I had power that my family members did not and do not have access to. At first I didn't want this power—I wanted to return to Mexico and reclaim my roots and plead with people to see me as a Mexican woman, but I also saw how unbelievably unrealistic this was. I was no longer the same girl that left Michoacan at seven years old. Although I was beginning to connect to a queer-people-of-color community, I was still killing myself with addiction to try and fit into American culture. By the time I was twenty-four I had heart and liver complications related to drug abuse. I was literally dying.

Transforming is not easy. For me it took a hitting a bottom, losing connection to people who loved me and could no longer tolerate my manipulative behaviors (because of my addiction) for me to change. But what came with that slow and painful change stays with me. In my sobriety I have more time to devote to my passions, and I am passionate about liberation. We need to envision new ways to believe in the possibility of freedom from all oppression. I do not believe that striving for and gaining power will dismantle the systems of power that exclude people. I have seen this reach and striving for power in my own family. Some of mis primos refuse to speak Spanish even if a newly migrated family member cannot understand English. Some of mis primos with college educations put down those who don't have the option.

I used to believe that experiencing oppression somehow made us more compassionate to other people's struggles. I have learned that solidarity does not come naturally; we must work on embracing and including all marginalized people in our movements. When we don't work on being inclusive we default to excluding the people that we have privilege over. Often times this exclusion is played out in our humor and choice of put-downs. For example, I have progressive people in my life who use ableist language to express frustration or to shut people down.

I question why gay marriage is talked about as if it will solve various forms of oppression that impact LGBTQIA communities. The reference to gay marriage as the next Civil Rights Movement is flawed. More energy should be put into making sure that the most vulnerable LGBTQIA members get basic needs met, such as securing more housing for homeless youth, ending violence towards transgender women, and providing queer immigrants with resources and support to prevent deportation. I don't see the same energy put into caring for our elders and people with disabilities, for community-run rehabilitation centers for addicts and alcoholics. The exclusion and afterthought of the most vulnerable of the LGBTQIA community is the reason I am not in support of gay marriage. I do not believe in centering the most powerful as a strategy in social change. I believe that it might shift the way people talk about an issue, but after a while the powerful have to find more micro-aggressive ways of keeping power and keeping it exclusive.

I know that gay marriage will help some people. For example, I know that it will allow some parents to have an easier, more secure life. But I still don't think it is enough. I worry the LGBTQIA community is depleting resources for a cause that will become a pinnacle of progress, a point of reference to demonstrate that everyone is equal.

Today I am set on not getting married unless it will save someone's life, by either preventing deportation or making sure that a child has secure guardianship. Although I am monogamous, and I want kids and I want a partner, I want liberation more than marriage. I am very set on creating a life of love that is centered in honoring my indigenous P'urepecha roots. Diaspora has meant finding home in my passions and drive for liberation for all. Being a witness to the stories that women in my family shared gave me a powerful lesson, that healing is possible and that we need each other to make it through struggle. It was then, in the kitchen, that I witnessed solidarity. The elders did the light work, the able-bodied kneaded the masa, and those who could not contribute were still part of the talk. Here academic language wasn't needed to communicate that we are valued, and that we can really be there for each other. For this and many other reasons I will no longer engage in single-issue struggles. These struggles, the one for gay marriage included, have often excluded me or people like me. I do not believe in an allegiance to scarcity, in fighting for a power that will only benefit a select few.

Penny Guisinger

Six-Point Win

It took twenty minutes to wash off the mud. It was caked on the shovel, the rake, my black rubber boots. Both pitchforks were coated, and I worked the hose down the length of each thin tine, chasing clumps of mud and grass until they flew off the pointy tips. The mud was thick, like clam-flat mud, but was instead from our garden, and it adhered to the soles of my boots like epoxy. We had spent the afternoon hauling seaweed, one wheelbarrow load at a time, across the muddy expanse of where the potatoes had grown, preparing the land for winter. Putting the garden to bed. The seaweed was part of the mess, skewered by the tip of the spade and the pitchforks. The force of the water wasn't enough to loosen it, so I pinched its rubbery strands between my gloved fingers and yanked it free, dropping it to the ground. It smelled like salt.

I want to tell you that the person working next to me was my wife, but our status had been made uncertain by the election.

Rather, the election—just four days prior—had failed to clar-
ify what we were to each other. Citizens of our state had gone
to the ballot box, slid their paper ballots through slots in heavy
wooden boxes or touched the screens of suspicious-looking machines, and weighed in with their opinions about our family. By
all objective measures, we won. My right to have a wife, instead of
a husband, was upheld with a six-point lead statewide. (No, not
in this town. Not on this rural, easternmost tip of the state. We
lost badly around here.) Our ceremony—the first one—was conducted down in Massachusetts, where we are legal. It might take a
couple of months, perhaps a court decision or two, to determine
if she was now my wife here at home too. Working next to me,
wearing a baseball cap and pink rubber boots, she was doing her
share to build this thing with me. This garden. This life.

Hosing off the trailer, trying to rinse off the salt, I drenched
myself and everything I was wearing. The frigid water—held
there by wet denim—chilled my skin. Last weekend, before the
election, we had hauled two trailer loads of salty rockweed, from
the beach by the state park, and dumped them next to the garden
fence. A friend—a man who knows about metals and things with
wheels—advised us to rinse our steel trailer after hauling a load
like that. "That salt water will eat right through the deck," he said.
"Get out the hose." I aimed the spray into each corner, trying to
get the corrosives out, trying to stave off damage.

It was an ugly campaign season. Right before the election,
we went to the mailbox to find a glossy flyer from the Maine
Republican Party, which made it clear that Mitt Romney and Paul
Ryan didn't approve of our family. "Marriage is one man, one
woman." The text was in a blocky, white font across the candidates'
black suits. "President Obama is too liberal for rural Maine." A
grainy photo of the president floated above those words. He had a
pinched, uncertain expression on his face. I wondered if it quali-
fied as hate mail. I wondered if I could sue the Maine Republican

Party for emotional damages. For sending hate mail to our house. For making us feel targeted, like political quarry.

The mud had worked its way into the tiny space between the shovel-head and the handle. I jammed the nozzle as firmly into that hole as I could, and the spray that erupted around it soaked my leather work gloves. I love wearing work gloves—love them for the generic quality they bring to my hands: When I wear work gloves, I work. I haul firewood or dig out the garlic bed or turn the compost pile or hitch my steel trailer up for a day of moving something around. They could be anyone's gloved hands as I look at them there on the handle of the shovel. They could be my father's. Or my wife's. Or one of the many neighbors who voted against us—neighbors who also spent that weekend putting their gardens to bed. We all prepared soil, planned ahead, made amendments that would help. As the blasting cold water cleared the tiny space between shovel-head and handle, as the water ran from muddy to clear, I wondered how the people of Maryland, Minnesota, and Washington were faring on this post-election Sunday. They must have soil to prepare. And mud to clean off their tools.

We carried the seaweed from its place by the fence, pushing it in a red wheelbarrow, now glazed with salt and mud, until we had moved it all. Beneath the two loads from last weekend was a smaller load from late September. It had been decomposing there across all those weeks, waiting to be moved into the garden. As our pitchforks dipped into that layer, it released a smell that we won't soon forget—rotted ocean stuff, the very depths of the sea turning to compost next to our garden fence. We moved it anyway. Its consistency was that of very fresh cow manure, pancake batter, pie filling. It made sloppy sounds as it landed on the soil, launched from our pitchforks. It was the messiest stuff, but we knew it contained the richest potential. We dug in, turning our heads to the sides to breathe as we worked. This would pay off.

Three years ago—the last time Maine voted on our marriage—a woman we know wrote a letter to the editor of our local newspaper. We don't know her well, but she's a local person, and all local people around here know each other a little bit. She's a writer. Considers herself a teacher. Teaches others how to write, or tries to. In her letter, she called our marriage a "social experiment" and urged everyone to cast ballots against us. We must have felt dangerous to her. Terrifying. It makes us laugh, and it also makes us avoid eye contact with her when we see her at the farmer's market. That was three years ago. We still avoid eye contact. Some mud, when it gets into places, doesn't wash out easily. We don't have that kind of power-washing equipment. Just a garden hose. It's not enough.

A six-point win is a clean margin. Decisive. That we lost by a twenty-point margin here in our home county is lost on the national news. It is not reported by Nate Silver or anyone else that when I drive my kids to school, I know which houses had signs campaigning against us planted on their lawns. All the well-intentioned straight people who clap us on the back and ask us when the wedding is have already tossed the hate mail in the recycling. I still have mine hidden on the phone table. In my head, I'm still writing the revenge letter that will accompany it back to the Maine Republican Party headquarters. Next week. When I have the strength, maybe. Or the time. When I'm done rinsing off the muck. When my boots are clean.

The patch of garden where we grew potatoes is the muddiest. That corner needs the most amending, needs an infusion of organic material—seaweed, compost—to transform the clay into soil. The potatoes didn't do well. Their dark, wrinkly leaves were consumed by an infestation of striped beetles that turned to neon orange smudges on our gloves when we removed and crushed them. We tried to keep up, but when our backs were turned, they stripped each potato plant down to its stem, forcing an early harvest of bite-sized potatoes. We've been told that healthy soil will fend off ugly attacks. That's what the experts say. Amend the soil. Add nutrients. Stir. Wait.

A straight friend, who'd moved from New York to Oregon last year, said to me before the election, "There are so many gay people out here, it's like everyone is just over it. They don't even hold pride parades or whatever anymore." My other Oregon friend, the gay one, saw her marriage dissolved when Oregon passed a constitutional amendment banning their already performed marriage. It was like losing her wife. I told the first friend that I thought maybe they needed a few more parades out there after all. She didn't even know. She couldn't smell it. It wasn't on her own skin.

From our dining room window, the half of the garden that is tucked in beneath a layer of rockweed looks like freshly tilled earth. The black sea plants—snaky vines and bubbly, finger-shaped leaves—mimic the beautifully lumpy look of fertile soil. From a distance, it's all a six-point, four-state win. From a distance, it's all beautiful potential.

Minh Pham

Bê Đê Pride

On Sunday, August 5, 2012, over a hundred bikers and motorcy-clists, with rainbow flags in their hands and colored paint on their faces, rode through the streets of Hanoi for Vietnam's first gay pride parade. It was a small parade. The streets were narrow, and the sidewalks were even narrower. There was barely enough space for two motorcycles to ride side by side.

The marchers did not obtain a permit for the parade. There was no support from the police. But there was no resistance from the police either. They allowed the parade to proceed.

Just a month before the parade, the prime minister of Vietnam received a proposal to include same-sex marriage in his coun-try's doctrine. He responded positively, affirming the reality of the growing numbers of gay couples, and stating that the only issues left to address were legal ones. If the proposal is adopted, Vietnam will be the first Asian country to allow same-sex marriage.

I was a graduate student at UC Riverside when I read about these events on Facebook. It came as a shock because I thought it would be decades before my birth country would make such a leap forward in gay acceptance.

My father took me to a wedding in Saigon when I was five. The streets were covered with red firecracker shells and yellow chrysanthemum petals.

Walls of people lined the streets, and my father lifted me onto his shoulders so I could watch the ceremony. I plugged my ears to muffle the loud pops from the firecrackers, red fish tails of bursting Tootsie Roll-sized papers.

The bride wore a red áo dài, a silk dress with long slits on both sides running up to her hip. For the wedding, the dress was decorated with an embroidered phoenix. Her father stood next to her with a smile and waited for the groom's family to arrive. In Vietnam it is tradition that the groom walk from his house to the bride's house to ask her parents for her hand in marriage.

When the groom entered the street, more firecrackers were lit. The groom's family carried red metal tins with fruit, rice wine, and tobacco leaves to offer to the bride's ancestors.

Everyone cheered. The groom wore a black French tuxedo.

My father pressed his elbows against my legs so that I wouldn't fall and clapped along with the crowd. He looked so happy for the new couple.

We had known the groom for years; he had helped build our house.

Within the same year, my mother and my aunts started pressuring my uncle to get married. People in the neighborhood were spreading rumors about him because he was a twenty-year-old man who had never shown any interest in girls, other than gossiping with them over a cup of artichoke tea.

One night, I heard my mother's voice coming from my

grandfather's attic. She and my three aunts were yelling at my uncle after he invited a man home for dinner.

"That bóng lại cái does not belong in our house," my mother said. "You will not bring him home again."

I did not understand what bóng lại cái meant, but I knew from the tone of my mother's voice that it was bad.

My uncle whispered something about loving the man.

"You will not," my mother said. "Ông Trời, God, will smite the whole family because of you."

I was afraid to venture up the stairs, into the attic, but I wanted to see if my uncle was okay.

When I got to the attic, he was crying in the corner. I could barely see him. The four women surrounded him in candlelight.

My mother called him bê đê because he loved a man.

I thought I might be bê đê as well.

In sixth grade, shortly after my family moved to America, my father and I began to drift apart. One reason was that I began to be attracted to boys. I would chase them down the soccer field, acting like I was blocking them from getting the ball. But I only chased the attractive ones.

Then, in seventh grade, I was involved in an accident. I had knelt at the side of the street to tie my shoelaces when a truck ran over the curb and me, crushing both of my legs in the process. My right leg was broken and my left needed skin grafts. To take care of me, my father quit his job as a cook at a Chinese restaurant. He stayed home for a year and helped me learn how to walk again. After I recovered, he had difficulty finding another job and instead did charity work at a Buddhist temple. He spent most of his time in the temple, helping the monks with small carpentry tasks. He said that he did it so that nothing bad would ever happen to me again.

I always knew my father loved me. When I needed skin grafts

after the accident, he asked the doctor to take skin from his legs instead of mine so I wouldn't go through any more pain. He left work early to pick me up from school. He said my grandfather was proud of me. I knew that was his way of saying he was proud of me too.

But we grew distant when he began to make homophobic slurs in front of me. He never directed them toward me—I wasn't out back then—but I always took it that way.

"Those bê đês should kill themselves and burn in hell," he would say, whenever there was an article about gay people in a Vietnamese newspaper. "Maybe it's good that they get AIDS so that they can all die off."

When I heard him say these things, I sat quietly next to him. I could see his anger through the red complexion of his face.

When I was seventeen, I went to college in Davis, California, five hundred miles away from my family's home in Riverside, in part because I wanted to have the freedom to explore my sexuality. My father's views remained unchanged, even as I visited home during the summer and holidays.

I told myself it was not my father's fault that he said those hurtful things. I blamed his words on the PTSD he had developed during the Vietnam War and from the years he spent in a reeducation camp.

But after many years, I could no longer lie to myself, and I accepted that the words came from him, not his PTSD, and that he meant what he said.

Ông Nội, my paternal grandfather, gave me a gold wedding band when I was nineteen. The band fit perfectly on my ring finger. My fifth aunt said he had measured the ring just by looking at my hand. She also said that he wanted me to marry a girl before he died.

I thought about giving him back the ring because I could not give him what he wanted. I was nineteen and had barely started college. I had never thought about marriage before. I knew I could not bring home the bride that he wanted.

I told him I could not keep his ring.

He folded the wedding band back into my hand and said, "I gave it to you so it could bring you happiness. I am proud of you."

My mother cried when I told her that I was gay. I told her a few days after I turned twenty, when I flew to Riverside to celebrate my birthday.

There was less risk in telling my mother. I always thought my father would be the first to know because we used to be so close when we were in Vietnam. I was afraid if I told him he would no longer be proud of me and would no longer accept me as his son.

My mother sat on the toilet and cried all night. She thought I was going to die. It was inevitable that I would get AIDS, she said.

One of her coworkers had told her about her own son, also gay. He always came by the nail shop to ask his mother for money. My mother said he looked sick, with rashes on his cheeks. She said he had AIDS.

It took my mother two years before she would talk to me again about my homosexuality.

"How are you going to have kids?" she asked.

I told her I was going to marry my partner and we would look into artificial insemination.

"Two men don't marry each other. That is not right," she said.

Our conversation ended there.

My mother's words left me disturbed. A week later I sat her down in the living room while my father slept.

"I told you that I was gay because I love you."

My mother remained quiet.

"I want you in my life."

My mother said that it would be hard for her to understand, but she would try.

In 2013, the *New York Times* published an article titled "Real Faces, Real People, Real Love in Vietnam." Pictures taken by Maika Elan, a Vietnamese photographer, accompanied the article, showing Vietnamese LGBTQ couples displaying intimacy behind closed doors. In one picture two gentlemen bathe each other using plastic pails. In another a son kisses his mother's partner's forehead while she rests in bed.

The article brought hope that Vietnam is becoming more accepting of gays. I imagine holding hands with my partner while walking down the streets of Saigon. I imagine my family acknowledging my gay uncle.

But as the article stated, these are photographs of gay love behind closed doors.

Visiting Vietnam in 2012, after its first pride parade, I thought there would be more respect shown to LGBTQ individuals, but not much had changed. People shook their heads in disappointment when my uncle displayed his feminine swagger on the streets of Saigon. Younger relatives I suspected to be gay were still being pushed into arranged marriages. Rainbow flags had not replaced communist flags.

I heard from my mother that my uncle's life revolves around selling knockoff Gucci bags at outdoor swap meets and helping tourists plan trips to Buddhist temples.

My mother said that my aunts forced him to go to temple. They thought his gayness could be expunged through hundreds of hours of prayers.

He was always cheerful, making me giggle anytime we were together during my last two visits to Vietnam. I thought my uncle knew I was like him, especially during my last visit, which happened after I had already come out to my mother.

There is a difference between someone thinking you are gay because they suspect it versus someone knowing you are gay because you have told them. I thought that if my uncle suspected I was gay, he would become closer to me, but if I directly told him I was gay, he might leak it in a conversation.

He is known to have a mouth on him, with no filter. During my first visit to Vietnam, when I was eighteen, he was introducing me around our neighborhood. We visited my childhood friend's house, and I didn't recognize my friend. I had last seen him when I was eight, before my family moved to America.

"Isn't he handsome?" my uncle blurted to me.

I looked at the ground, my smile not visible to anyone.

I could not even tell my uncle because, at the time, I was scared of being rejected by my own family. I imagined gaining riches or fame or success and then coming out to everyone. My family would be speechless because I would have brought pride to them. And this pride would outweigh the loss of face that comes from having a gay person in the family.

The Santa Ana Tết festival, held every Lunar New Year, hosts the largest Vietnamese parade in California. In 2010 an LGBTQ group called the Viet Rainbow of Orange County (VROC) began marching in the Tết parade.

I first heard about this on the radio, on a trip to Santa Ana for my twentieth birthday dinner, as my father drove. I was happy to hear that LGBTQ people were being included in the Vietnamese American community, but all I remembered was my father talking over the radio.

"Who the hell let those fags walk in the parade?" he said.

I sat quietly in the back.

In 2012, due to budget cuts, control of the parade passed from the city to a community organization called the Vietnamese American Federation of Southern California. One of their first steps was to exclude VROC from marching in the parade, on the grounds that being gay was "not part of the Vietnamese culture."

VROC members and supporters fought this action in court. After a year, a compromise was reached; the final decision would be left to a vote of community leaders.

The gays won, by a margin of fifty-one to thirty-six, with ten abstentions. Among those who voted in favor were the South Vietnamese Marines Veteran Charities Association and the Union of Vietnamese Student Associations of Southern California.

On February 1, 2014, VROC marched with seventy-four other groups in the Tết parade, carrying rainbow flags without any opposition.

Recently, I have discovered more LGBTQ members in my family.

My female second cousin likes girls.

I think her nephew is also gay. He sashays around, like my uncle. He speaks quietly, like my uncle. Not the quiet that comes from being shy, but the quiet that comes from being afraid of saying things that will cause others to beat him.

My fifth aunt has a daughter. During my last trip back, my cousin Bi was very attached to me. I didn't think anything about it. But on my visit last year, I understood better why.

My mother and I found out on our visit to my Aunt Hồng's house, located just outside Saigon. On this visit Aunt Hồng's step-aunt also joined us for lunch.

"Your niece is different," Aunt Hồng said to my mother. "She might be sick. She keeps taping down her breasts."

"She's not sick," the stepaunt said. "She's just different."

"When did this start?" my mother asked.

"Three years ago, when her breasts came in," Aunt Hồng said.

"Is it because she's gay?" my mother asked.

"No, I don't think so. She told me she sees herself as a boy, not a girl," the stepaunt said.

"How can she think she's a boy? She was born a girl," Aunt Hồng said, her voice breaking.

She excused herself by carrying dirty dishes to the kitchen.

On the taxi ride back I told my mom that it would be better if Bi came to America. I could take my cousin to the LGBTQ center to make friends. My mother nodded.

On my father's side, my male cousin Hải was being forced into marriage.

My father's side of the family lives in the farmland near Cần Thơ, two hours south of Saigon. People in the farmland are less open about homosexuality than people in the city. Before my mother and I traveled to the farmland to visit, she told me to man up—to hide my jazz hands and keep my mouth from running like a gossiping grandma on mahjong night.

Hải was thirty-three. People were starting to question why he hadn't married yet. He was tall and had a big build, unlike the other men in my family, who are skinny like coconut trees. He was a chemical engineer who studied in Saigon. I wondered if Hải had moved to Saigon to study so he could be free to live an alternate life.

The fact that he was thirty-three and had never had a girlfriend made me suspect he was gay.

One night, I was playing cards with my male cousins, and a neighborhood girl joined in. My cousins began to make fun of Hải by nudging him toward the girl. The more cousins that joined in on the joke, the more uncomfortable he looked.

On the bus back to Saigon, I asked my mother about Hải.

"Your aunt has arranged for Hải to get married next year," my mother said.

"I think Hải is gay," I said.

"I think so, too."

"Isn't it sad?" I said.

"You know how your aunt is. She would get her grandchild even if she had to stand outside their room on their honeymoon."

A year and a half after my grandfather gave me his wedding ring, I heard that he had lung cancer. He kept his pain a secret for years. None of his children or grandchildren knew. But after ten years of smoking, his right lung decayed to mush. It became so painful that he finally told one of my aunts to take him to the doctor. The doctor said that it was too late. The cancer had already spread.

I remembered he gurgled when he coughed. But I didn't know it was cancer.

He climbed up a mountain to a Buddhist temple with me the last time I visited. At ninety, he was strong enough to climb up the steps with his wooden cane. Before I left to go back to America, I asked him to stop smoking so he would still be alive the next time I visited. He told me he would if I did well in school.

A year later, my father flew back to Vietnam to be by my grandfather's side. My parents kept his condition a secret from me because they didn't want it to affect my education. When he was close to dying, my mother called and told me, and I yelled at her. I wanted to go back to Vietnam, but she said we did not have enough money and he would not want me to drop out.

When I called my grandfather's house, my fifth aunt picked up. As my aunt passed the phone to my grandfather, I could hear him tell my aunt that he did not want me to know he was in pain. He told me that he loved me and that he was proud.

"Con thương Ông Nội. I love you, Grandpa," I replied.

Three days later, I got a frantic call from my mother telling me that my grandfather was dying. I called as quickly as I could. The first time no one picked up. The second time no one picked up. The third time my father got hold of the phone.

"Son, Ông Nội has passed," he said.

I cried. "But—but Mom just said that he was dying. I called back right away."

"I'm sorry," he said. "Ông Nội told me to tell you this: do well in school, don't do drugs…"

He paused. "And don't become gay."

I stopped crying. I knew that my grandfather would never have said that to me.

I called my mother and told her what my father had told me, and I asked her if my grandfather would have said such a thing. She confirmed my suspicion that he altered my grandfather's last words in an attempt to change me.

I twisted my grandfather's ring off my finger and secured it on my Buddha necklace to save for my wedding day. I whispered some prayers for my grandfather.

By coming to America, I could live a life as a gay man.

My mother told me that she and my father gave up their lives so that my brother and I could receive an education in America.

The Việt Cộng put my father into a reeducation camp for over seven years because he fought alongside the Americans during the Vietnam War. He was imprisoned for another two and a half years because he tried to flee the country by boat with my family. They released my mother because my older brother had recently been born.

My mother dropped out of a prelaw program in college and sold cigarettes on the streets of Saigon to make enough money to keep my father alive in camp and to keep her eight siblings and my older brother fed. I was born after my father was released from prison, ten years after the Vietnam War ended.

My mother said if I had stayed in Vietnam, my fate would have been to sell lottery tickets in the streets or to make carpentry nails in a factory.

Growing up, my parents pushed me to excel in America so that I could have a successful career and a good life for my future family.

I am the second oldest son in my family. All of my relatives in Vietnam expect me to achieve greatness. My grandfather, when giving me my wedding band, expected me to represent my family name. But my personal goal when I came to America was to raise a family with another man. Only then would I find the greatness that they sought.

My father still cannot accept me as a man because I am gay.

One day I will get married. I hope he can understand before then.

Joseph Nicholas DeFilippis

Wedding Bells Are Breaking Up That Old Gang of Mine

The Loss of Legal Protections for LGBT Families in the Wake of Gay Marriage Victories

Luis and Tommy: Friends with Benefits

Luis and Tommy are gay men who met at work when they were in their mid-forties, and have been best friends for twenty-seven years. When they turned sixty, they decided to become room-mates so they could take care of each other as they aged. For over a decade now, they have shared the costs of rent, utilities, and food. They share one car and its related expenses. When Tommy had pneumonia, Luis drove him to the doctor. When Luis developed cancer, Tommy went with him to each of his chemo sessions. They are registered as domestic partners in Oregon and have drawn up paperwork giving each other power of attorney to make financial and medical decisions if either of them becomes incapacitated. These two men do not have any connection by blood, nor are they romantically involved, but they are family by any definition that matters to me.

I spent five years as the director of SAGE/Queens, an organization serving LGBT senior citizens, the majority of whom live alone without children to help support them as they age. Yet in my work, I saw firsthand the numerous ways in which LGBT people created unique forms of family. I saw friends form care-giving groups when one of them was sick. I saw neighbors make up schedules to take turns doing shopping when one of them was homebound. Most of these relationships had no legal protection, but a few of them were registered as domestic partners.

Tommy and Luis have no desire to be married to each other, or romantically involved, but they registered as domestic partners in order to get the legal and economic benefits that come with it. Yet if Oregon legalizes gay marriage, Tommy and Luis might lose these benefits.

Gay Marriage: The Limiting of Options

The definitions of domestic partnerships vary from city to city. Most offer access to the state-level government rights, benefits, and responsibilities of marriage. Some state governments—such as California, Nevada, Oregon, and Washington—offer more complete relationship recognition than other states—such as Hawaii, Maine, Maryland, and Wisconsin, for example—where benefits are more limited.

I live in Oregon, where same-sex marriage became legal earlier this year. I have spoken to staff, volunteers, and board members of Basic Rights Oregon (BRO), the statewide equality organization and one of the organizations leading the fight for marriage equality, and I have repeatedly asked what will happen to Oregon's domestic partnerships now that same-sex marriage is legal; no one from BRO has any idea. As I'm writing this, their website and the websites for their partner organizations Freedom to Marry, Human Rights Campaign, and Oregon United for Marriage make no mention of the future of domestic partnerships in Oregon.

A look to our neighbor in the Pacific Northwest provides a clue about one potential outcome. In 2012, gay marriage was approved in Washington State when Governor Christine Gregoire signed a bill that had been passed by the state legislature; voters later approved the legislation in a statewide referendum. By the end of the year, a new law went into effect, automatically converting all of Washington's domestic partnerships into marriages on June 30, 2014, unless the domestic partnerships were proactively dissolved first. Now that same-sex couples have the right to get married, Washington will no longer offer domestic partnerships.

The Washington law is the natural outgrowth of a decade-long trend. In 2004, when Massachusetts became the first state to issue marriage licenses to same-sex couples, local businesses soon eliminated domestic partnership benefits. When Connecticut and New Hampshire passed same-sex marriage laws, all same-sex civil unions were converted into marriages. In 2011, when New York State approved same-sex marriage, schools in Westchester County ended their domestic partnership benefits and began requiring their employees get married or else lose the ability to provide their benefits to their partners.

These decisions are predicated on the assumption that the only reason to offer domestic partnerships was that same-sex couples could not marry. In this framework, a domestic partnership is viewed as a consolation prize for same-sex couples who would rather get married. Indeed, the very first sentence on Freedom to Marry's page about civil unions and domestic partnership reads "civil union and domestic partnerships are a second-class status."[i] This perspective fails to recognize the possibility that for many families, domestic partnership and civil unions are preferable to marriage.

Domestic Partnerships: Not Merely a Second-Class Marriage

Domestic partner (DP) benefits were created due to cultural shifts in the 1960s and 1970s. Women were working outside the home and less dependent on a husband for an income, premarital sex gained cultural acceptance, no-fault divorces were created, and the country saw reductions in the legal and social stigmas against children born outside of marriage.[ii] These changes resulted in the diminished legal importance of marriage, and eventually employers began to provide benefits that were not dependent upon marriage. In 1982, the New York City weekly newspaper the *Village Voice* became the first employer to provide domestic partner benefits to unmarried couples, and three years later the city of Berkeley, California, became the first public employer to offer domestic partnership benefits. Different-sex and same-sex couples were both eligible for these benefits, despite the revisionist history now offered by marriage equality activists who claim that domestic partnerships were always a watered-down status for gay couples who could not marry. Over the next decade, businesses and municipalities across the country began offering DP benefits to their unmarried employees—gay or straight. These employers understood that the American family was changing, and that many people were building family outside of marriage. These families included same-sex couples, but also included different-sex couples that had the right to marry but could not or did not want to do so.

Unfortunately, in the '90s, this began to change and some

employee health benefits became limited *only* to same-sex partners. Since then, companies have been split about whether domestic partnership was offered to heterosexual couples. Today, some states (Colorado, Illinois, and Hawaii) allow both same-sex and different-sex couples to enter into civil unions, and other places (Nevada and the District of Columbia) allow different-sex couples to enter an equivalent status, which they call domestic partnership. Nevertheless, in recent years many places have restricted civil unions and domestic partnerships to same-sex couples, forcing different-sex couples to get married if they wish to access benefits. This change has limited the options available to alternative family structures. The result is that a policy that was originally conceived in response to the reduced importance of marriage and as a means of providing benefits to unmarried people has become a policy that supports the dominance of marriage, except now it includes same-sex couples.

Yet, the cultural shifts of the 1960s and '70s have not been reversed: marriage continues to be less significant to the formation and structure of families. Consequently, compulsory marriage is not the way to protect our families. After all, the majority of domestic partnerships are actually held by heterosexual couples that have the legal right to marry but—for whatever reason—choose not to.[iii] Are these couples to be thrown under the bus in our pursuit of "gay equality"?

Household Diversity: The Norm, Not the Exception

In the last forty years, the number of US households consisting of married couples with children has been cut in half, and currently only one-fifth of households match the traditional notion of family defined as mother, father, and their biological children. Today, the majority of American households are structured differently—as single people, childless cohabitating couples, unmarried parents with children, single-parent households, grandparents raising their grandkids or other kinship care arrangements, queer parents, friends, multigenerational households, extended families, and blended families.

Marriage is no longer a requirement for child rearing. In 2008, almost twenty-two million children lived with one parent while the other parent lived somewhere else.[iv] Almost half of American children live with unmarried (but cohabiting) parents by age twelve, and one fourth of children live with a parent who is divorced.[v] While the country has undergone this radical shift in the actual makeup of our families, it seems ludicrous for marriage equality activists to continue to prop up the theoretical and legal primacy of marriage.

Family structures have also changed in other ways. In the last thirty years, technology has been created that aids or replaces various stages of insemination, conception, pregnancy, and childbirth. It is increasingly common for parents and their children to have long-term relationships with their sperm donors, surrogates, and egg donors, as well as with the spouses or children of those people. These complicated relationships fall outside the protection of marriage laws.

Parents are not the only ones raising children. In the United States, there are almost three million children living with relatives other than their parents,[vi] and over almost half a million children in foster care.[vii] In 2008, a record forty-nine million Americans lived in a multigenerational family household.[viii] The number of children living in grandparent-headed households has doubled in the last few decades, and at the start of the twenty-first century approximately 2.4 million grandparents were the primary caregivers of their grandchildren.[ix] How exactly is it helpful to these millions of children to make marriage the only legitimate form of family that deserves legal protection?

Being considered a family does not require the presence of children. In 2012, the Census Bureau reported 6.8 million different-sex unmarried couples were cohabiting in the United States. Sixty percent of those couples had no children living with them.[x] It is time we complicated the dominant cultural narrative that families are defined by the act of raising children.

Women live longer than men, and since 1990, the number of women over fifty who divorce has doubled. Mobilized labor often requires that children move away from their parents for employment purposes, and these children are often not present to help care for them as they age. As a result, four million US women over fifty live not with their husbands or children, but in households with at least two other women also aged over fifty, in a "Golden Girls" type of arrangement.[xi] This statistic is expected to rise as the baby boomer generation continues to age.

All of the families described above illustrate how modern American life no longer resembles the traditional "mom, dad, and the kids" image that we continue to pretend is the norm. None of these family configurations are defined by marriage, and none of them receive the same legal protections as married couples.

LGBT Families: Additional Family Formations

It is obvious that heterosexual families are created in ways that make legal marriage an insufficient means by which to disperse protections and rights. LGBT families share the same dynamics and structures described above, but are also complicated in additional ways. Forced to live outside the law for so many decades, LGBT people had to get very creative in composing our families.

Many same-sex couples have had children via adoption, but many other LGBT people have become parents in other ways, which have been documented by activist Terry Boggis. It is not unusual for a gay man and a lesbian to conceive and co-parent children together, or for a gay couple and a lesbian couple to co-parent as four parents (when the law only recognizes two of them as the legal guardians).

LGBT parents utilize alternative methods of conception perhaps more frequently than do heterosexuals. For instance, lesbian couples often use sperm donors, and increasingly, these donors are remaining actively involved in the children's lives. Queer people have used "adopted" embryos, sometimes co-parenting with the heterosexual couple that generated the embryo. In addition, gay men often hire surrogates who may remain in the child's life.

In LGBT communities there is also a long tradition of ex-lovers remaining central in each other's lives, making divorce and remarriage even more complicated than it is among heterosexual couples. There are countless LGBT families with multiple moms and dads "due to separation, partner changing or blending, and the endless redefinition and shape-shifting nature of real family relationships, where some people stay and others sometimes go." [xii]

In addition, LGBT people often create families that are not centered on parenting and marriage. Numerous complicated family forms have been created, both inside and outside of existing legal frameworks. Young queer people of color still create family structures in the different Houses of the ballroom scene, where they live together under one roof, under the care of a maternal figure.[xiii] Some LGBT adults exist in long-term, committed, polyamorous relationships. LGBT people are also more likely than their heterosexual siblings to be responsible for taking in an aging parent to care for them,[xiv] making multigenerational households more common. For the past three decades we have seen the creation of long-term caregiving relationships that provide support to those living with extended illness such as HIV/AIDS. And increasingly, LGBT senior citizens have created Gay "Golden Girls" arrangements, living together and sometimes making legal contracts to care for each other.

I know six women who have made such a contract. Cathy, Helen, Kim, and Paula are four lesbian senior citizens who are close friends. Together with Helen's mother and Cathy's sister (both of whom are straight women), the six decided to become legal caregivers and decision-makers for each other. They searched for months until they found a building where they could get apartments next door to each other, and then moved in so that they (like Luis and Tommy) could be close by to take care of each other. Then they went one step further than Luis and Tommy and hired a lawyer. They spent more months, and many dollars, drawing up legal documents (which they had to create themselves, since there was no existing template) that name all six of them as legally responsible for each other until death.

Outside the Law: The Limitations of Family Recognition

There are no existing legal frameworks for any of the relationships described above; they remain unprotected in court and unsupported by government programs. Your best friend is not eligible to receive your Social Security benefits, regardless of how long she may have been living with and caring for you. To protect these kinds of families we need more legal options, not fewer. Winning gay marriage only benefits a small percentage of queer people, and doing away with domestic partnerships, civil unions, or reciprocal beneficiaries actually hurts many families, gay and straight. Marriage is not the only valuable form of family or relationship, and it should not be economically and legally privileged above all others.

We must reframe "marriage equality" in terms of the right to form a family and share household resources inside and outside marriage, instead of focusing exclusively on the right of gay and lesbian couples to marry. Rather than fighting for marriage, we should have a broader vision and must expand our fight to include legal recognition for many kinds of relationships, households, and families, regardless of conjugal status or kinship. The creativity and ingenuity that queer people have shown in creating multiple kinds of families have been profoundly absent from the vision of national LGBT organizations, which should be protecting the many family formations that we actually live in instead of proposing that the way to get rights is to live as a romantic couple and get married. We must also fight for access for all people, regardless of marital status, to vital government support programs such as Social Security or health care. Marriage should not be the vehicle through which legal rights and government benefits are distributed.

Beyond Marriage: Other Models Do Exist

Hospitals typically grant husbands or wives the power to make medical decisions for their incapacitated spouses if there is not documentation indicating otherwise. Yet, a study conducted in Chicago showed that 33 percent of married people would choose someone other than their spouse to make medical decisions for them, while a similar study in Detroit found that 50 percent of married people wanted someone other than their spouse to do this.[xv] Why does marriage continue to be our legal default? Not just for medical decision-making, but in general, might other options be preferable for everyone? The rights, privileges, and responsibilities that come with marriage might be better dispersed by either individualizing them (allow people to self-determine who makes their medical decisions) or universalizing them (national health care for all, rather than having to marry someone for their employee benefits). There are already such policies in place, both abroad and at home, from which we can learn.

Numerous other countries have begun to provide legal protections for families created outside of marriage. France has PACS, government-ordained civil unions allowing unmarried couples most of the tax benefits and legal protections of marriage, and they are very popular among both same-sex and different-sex couples. For over a decade, local governments in Australia have offered two distinct categories of registered partnership: "Significant Relationships" (same-sex and different-sex couples) and "Caring Relationships" (non-conjugal relationships between any two people where one provides the other with domestic help and personal care). Both types of relationships provide marriage-like rights regarding employment benefits, taxation, insurance, hospital visitation, health care, division of property, and wills.

Even marriage itself is not always so narrowly conceptualized overseas. In the Netherlands and Sweden, there are numerous forms of marriage, including spouses who live apart, and each form has a different legal name and status. By the beginning of the twenty-first century, Canada had essentially abandoned the legal distinctions between married and unmarried couples. Consequently, when same-sex marriage was passed, it became a symbolic option for couples that wanted to express their commitment; it was not required to obtain any rights or benefits, because they already had them. In the province of Alberta, family recognition is even more expansive: a legal status called "adult interdependent relationships" covers non-conjugal relationships (such as friends, cousins, siblings, etc.), providing them with certain legal and economic protections.

Here in the United States, we can find examples of legislation that provide piecemeal aspects of broader family recognitions. In 2004, California became the first of three states to provide partially paid family leave — an insurance program that provides income replacement to eligible workers for family caregiving for a parent, child, spouse or domestic partner, or to bond with a newborn or newly adopted child. A similar federal bill has been introduced, but has not yet passed. In September 2013, Governor Jerry Brown signed a bill expanding California's program to include caring for seriously ill grandparents, grandchildren, siblings, and parents-in-law. These policies are still based on marital status or kinship, but at least they have expanded the definition of family beyond just married couples and their children.

Some states—including Arizona, California, Idaho, Maryland, North Carolina, and Vermont—have advance directive registries where a person can designate whomever they want (spouse, lover, family, friend, roommate) to make medical decisions for them.[xvi] And when someone in West Virginia dies on the job, the state allows anyone who was "financially dependent" upon them to file a wrongful death suit, regardless of their relationship's marital status or romantic (or non-romantic) nature. Policies like these are mere examples of the kinds of starting points that can be used for building a larger agenda of more expansive family recognition legislation.

More recently, some states have created various legal statuses that allow individuals to determine their own beneficiaries or designees to receive government protections and benefits. Initially, the "reciprocal beneficiaries" status was offered in only two states—Hawaii and Vermont—to close relatives or friends and provided limited benefits, but this status made the sexual and romantic relationships of the recipients irrelevant, keeping the state out of the business of sexual regulation. Now, various municipalities (e.g., El Paso, New York City, Washington, D.C.) allow any two people who live together in a committed, familial relationship to enter a domestic partnership.

In 2006, Salt Lake City allowed city employees to identify an "adult designee" (any domestic partner, relative, or roommate with whom they are economically interdependent) who is entitled to health insurance benefits. This policy was created to avoid specific endorsement of same-sex couples, and as such, marriage equality advocates have criticized it for failing to validate their relationships. I have little patience for such arguments because the result of this policy is that more people, in romantic and non-romantic relationships, are eligible for health benefits than if the city had followed a marriage model via domestic partnerships dependent upon conjugal relationships. When a lawsuit was filed against the plan, the judge who upheld the law said "single employees may have relationships outside of marriage, whether motivated by family feeling, emotional attachment or practical considerations, which draw on their resources to provide the necessaries of life, including health care."[xvii] This kind of analysis recognizes the reality of American families, and this policy is easily replicable in other municipalities.

In 2009, the state of Colorado created a status called "designated beneficiaries," used to confer government protections and benefits to families. By completing one form, any two people can self-determine which legal rights and consequences they want to apply to their relationship. Options include receiving employee health care benefits, making heath care and burial decisions, serving as power of attorney, access to hospital or nursing home visitation, and inheritance. Each person can choose which rights and powers they want to give the other person (they don't even have to pick identical options) by simply marking the appropriate box. Such an adaptable set of options has the potential to revolutionize caregiving and family recognition in this country. The potential importance of replicating this plan across the country cannot be understated.

Expanding Family Recognition:
A Lesson From Across the Country

These kinds of policies can be achieved if we stay focused on the big picture and do not settle for short-term victories (with their "we'll come back for you later" strategies). We have to situate same-sex couples as one part of our LGBT communities, but not the only part. I offer the following example as an illustration of how more progressive wins are possible.

When I lived in New York City, I was the executive director of Queers for Economic Justice (QEJ) from 2003–2009. We spent over two years working on a campaign to get the City of New York's Department of Homeless Services (DHS) to change their policies about providing shelter for homeless domestic partners. When domestic partnership laws were passed in New York City over twenty years earlier, they included a list of city agencies that were required to treat domestic partners as if they were married. DHS was not included in that list of agencies. Consequently, DHS was separating homeless domestic partners who tried to access shelter and housing them in their "single adult" shelters, rather than housing them together in the "family" shelters (which were reserved for couples with marriage licenses). For years, same-sex domestic partners seeking to enter the NYC shelter system found themselves faced with a choice between being separated in the system or remaining together on the streets.

QEJ convened a coalition of various LGBT and homeless organizations to work together to force the city to allow domestic partners access to the family shelters. Early on, we were told by DHS officials that the issue was not homophobia, but rather fraud (by straight couples). They claimed that heterosexuals who were not actually couples were entering into fraudulent domestic partnerships in order to access the family shelters, which were "nicer" than the bleak single-adult shelters. They could not provide any evidence of this fraud. Eventually, in response to our protests, DHS proposed allowing couples with the "highest legally recognized form of documentation" to access the family shelters. This meant different-sex couples could not use domestic partnerships (they needed an actual marriage license) but same-sex couples could.

This led to one of the most difficult parts of the campaign. Empire State Pride Agenda, New York's statewide equality organization and the most politically influential LGBT group in the state, wanted to take this "win" for gay couples. QEJ and our other partner organizations argued that we should keep fighting and not "sell out" homeless straight couples. Difficult internal conversations ensued (highlighting our different agendas), but eventually everyone in our coalition agreed to keep fighting. We rejected DHS's offer.

We approached the New York City Council with the issue, and convinced them to draft a bill that would force the mayor to do what we sought. The result was far better than if we had accepted the initial offer. During our time lobbying government officials, we spoke to them about the complicated ways in which LGBT people create families. We had long conversations about the need for expanded family protections. Consequently, DHS now not only allows same-sex and different-sex couples to use DPs to access family housing, but the definition of family has been expanded. Because of our continued advocacy, the city's legal definition of family includes adults who are medically dependent upon one another or who share a caregiving relationship, including non-conjugal relationships, such as siblings, or aunts/uncles to nephews or nieces, or grandparents to grandchildren.

If we had listened to the statewide equality group who wanted to take the initial win for same-sex couples, we would have been granted access to the family shelters for same-sex couples, but we never would have achieved this expanded definition of family.

This victory took more time, but the result benefits far more people. This kind of policy is what is needed in municipalities across the country, and the equality groups in every state, as well as the national organizations who share their myopic concern for romantic couples, would be wise to take a lesson from this story.

Conclusion: Progressive Equality Means More than Marriage Equality

Progressive equality for all families is only possible by extricating marriage from benefits. Marriage should maintain its personal, cultural, emotional, and religious importance, and be celebrated in families, communities, and religious institutions. However, it should not grant access to government benefits. Instead of making marriage mandatory in order to access benefits, protections, and rights, we must provide options for different forms of households to fit government benefits to their changing needs. We need an adaptable variety of legal options to protect families, queer or straight, married or not. We must stop conferring a privileged status to marriage above all other family forms.

For years, many LGBT people have made this same argument. Prominent scholars (Cathy Cohen, John D'Emilio, Lisa Duggan, Nancy Polikoff, etc.), grassroots organizations (Against Equality, Audre Lorde Project, Queers for Economic Justice, etc.), community leaders (Terry Boggis, Kenyon Farrow, Amber Hollibaugh, Yasmin Nair, etc.), and countless LGBT bloggers and activists have long advocated for the separation of benefits from marriage and for the protection of multiple family structures. Yet these voices have been ignored, and often maligned, by the marriage equality leadership. The disastrous, infuriating result of ignoring them has been the rolling back of decades of progress. Now, in every state, we must fight all over again to reinstate or maintain domestic partnerships, civil unions, adult designees, and reciprocal beneficiaries. However, fighting to maintain (or reinstate) them is just the beginning; we must actually build on them and increase their legal power.

Washington State's decision to eliminate domestic partnerships is a great tragedy that must be reversed. As Oregon and other states wrestle with the legalization of same-sex marriage, each must recognize the diversity of its families, gay and straight, and choose to expand, rather than constrict, their legal options. Despite the claims of some marriage equality advocates, domestic partnership was never just a second-rate marriage in need of being replaced by full marriage rights. Domestic partnerships and other types of family recognition have the power to support many forms of family, beyond just same-sex couples. We must expand, rather than eliminate, these family protections, for the sakes of Tommy and Luis; for the sakes of Cathy, Helen, Kim, and Paula; and for millions of other households. Rather than making one-size-fits-all marriage compulsory, we must create additional means of protecting the odd, creative, and beautiful diversity of our queer families.

Notes

[i] Freedom to Marry, "Marriage vs. Civil Union or Domestic Partnership," (n/d), http://www.freedomtomarry.org/pages/marriage-versus-civil-unions-domestic-partnerships-etc.

[ii] Nancy D. Polikoff, "What Marriage Equality Arguments Portend for Domestic Partner Employee Benefits," NYU Review of Law and Social Change 37, no. 1 (2013): 49, http://socialchangenyu.files.wordpress.com/2013/03/37-1-polikoff.pdf.

[iii] Hewitt Associates, Survey Findings: Domestic Partners 2000, (Lincolnshire, IL: Hewitt Associates, 2000).

[iv] Timothy S. Grall, "Custodial Mothers and Fathers and Their Child Support: 2007," Current Population Reports (US Census Bureau: 2009), http://www.census.gov/prod/2009pubs/p60-237.pdf.

[v] Centers for Disease Control and Prevention, "National Survey of Family Growth," Centers for Disease Control and Prevention, (2011), http://www.cdc.gov/nchs/nsfg.htm.

[vi] Sara B. Eleoff, "American Academy of Pediatrics 2010 National Conference and Exhibition," Abstract 9042, (2010).

[vii] Centers for Disease Control and Prevention, "AFCARS (Adoption and Foster Care Analysis and Reporting System Report)," Centers for Disease Control and Prevention, (2011). Report.

[viii] Pew Research Center (2010). "The Return of the Multi-Generational Family Household," (Pew Research Center: 2010), http://www.pewsocialtrends.org/files/2010/10/752-multi-generational-families.pdf.

[ix] Hwa-Ok Park, "Grandmothers Raising Grandchildren: Family Well-being and Economic Assistance," *Focus 24*, no. 1 (2005): 19–27.

[x] US Census Bureau, "Profile America Facts for Features," US Census Bureau, (2012), http://www.census.gov/newsroom/releases/archives/facts_for_features_special_editions/cb12-ff18.html.

[xi] Sally Abrahms, "House Sharing for Boomer Women Who Would Rather Not Live Alone," *AARP Bulletin*, (AARP, May 2013), http://www.aarp.org/home-family/your-home/info-05-2013/older-women-roommates-house-sharing.html.

[xii] Terry Boggis, "Still Coming Ashore: The LGBT Community and the Many Meanings of Family," *A New Queer Agenda*, (S&F Online, Fall 2011/Spring 2012), http://sfonline.barnard.edu/a-new-queer-agenda/still-coming-ashore-the-lgbt-community-and-the-many-meanings-of-family/.

[xiii] Emily A. Arnold and Marlon M. Bailey, "Constructing Home and Family: How the Ballroom Community Supports African American GLBTQ Youth in the Face of HIV/AIDS," *Journal of Gay & Lesbian Social Services* 21, no. 2 (2009): 171–188.

[xiv] Mandy Hu, *Selling Us Short: How Social Security Privatization Will Affect Lesbian, Gay, Bisexual, and Transgender Americans*, (New York: National Gay and Lesbian Task Force Policy Institute, 2005), http://www.thetaskforce.org/downloads/reports/reports/SellingUsShort.pdf.

[xv] K Michael Lipkin, (2006). "Brief Report: Identifying a Proxy for Health Care as Part of Routine Medical Inquiry," *Journal of General Internal Medicine* 21, no. 11 (Nov 2006): 1188–1191. doi: 10.1111/j.1525-1497.2006.00570.x.

[xvi] Nancy D. Polikoff, *Beyond (Straight and Gay) Marriage: Valuing All Families Under the Law* (Boston: Beacon Press, 2008).

[xvii] American Civil Liberties Union of Utah, "Norman v. Anderson (2006)," ACLU of Utah, (May 2006), http://www.acluutah.org/legal-work/resolved-cases/item/178-norman-v-anderson/178-norman-v-anderson.

Meg Stone

We Have Cancer

I don't want us to spend the rest of our lives crediting cancer every time we follow our dreams, focus on what's really important, or devote our lives to service. We lived that way before Mal got sick.

Mal, my partner of fifteen years, used to be able to fill out medical history forms in two minutes. Nothing was ever wrong with her. She wasn't asthmatic or hypoglycemic, diabetic or allergic. Blood pressure, bone density, good. Cholesterol a little high but still normal. She got over a cold in a day and got out of bed the minute she woke up. While I spent the first years of our relationship visiting homeopaths and holistic doctors and Chinese herbalists hoping to cure my vague symptoms, she worked in a hospital with kids who were seriously sick.

She hated her periods. We fought when she made us skip a white-water rafting trip because she wouldn't wear a tampon. At the time I didn't appreciate how upset she was by biological imperatives that forced her out of the fluid space she occupies, the space between man and woman where neither or both of those labels fit. Those long, clotting, cramping periods kept her body from making sense. They forced her to reckon with uterus, cervix, vagina.

Mal is buzz-cut and freckled. She buys her jeans in the men's section and wears vintage 1950s belt buckles. Some straight people panic when they see her in the women's restroom. When children ask if she's a boy or a girl, she replies, "I'm me."

When the doctor diagnosed the period trouble as fibroid tumors, a problem that could be resolved with a hysterectomy, it was as if the riddle of Mal's body was solved. The biological destiny, the organ that shed its lining once a month to yank her back into the gender she was assigned at birth, could be pulled out through a small incision. Four weeks later she could start lifting weights again.

During the surgery I sat on the floor in the waiting room with my computer on my lap. I distracted myself with websites and blogs while Mal's mother and her best friend talked about tax policy. (Her mom was the first woman head of land assessment for the state. She rarely talks about anything else. Even with Mal in surgery.) The clock on my computer reminded me how long it had been since they wheeled her into the operating room. Almost two hours longer than they told me the surgery would take. Every time the door to the operating room opened I startled. Every time a doctor who wasn't ours emerged I got more scared.

"What's going on in there? They were supposed to be done by now," I said.

Mal's best friend put her hand on my arm. A television producer, she explained that sometimes shoots run long because they have to move all the lights. It doesn't mean anything's wrong, it just makes everything take longer. "Don't worry," she said. "They're just moving the lights."

I got jealous of the other people in the waiting room as doctors with pale green masks around their necks came out to tell them how successful the surgeries had gone. Most doctors stood with their patients' loved ones in the middle of the waiting room and gave reports that sounded almost casual. As if no crisis had been averted and no bad outcome was possible.

When Mal's surgeon finally emerged she invited us into a small conference room.

"This must be bad," I said. "Or you'd tell us in the waiting room."

The doctor assured me she was only respecting our privacy. She told us that a cyst on Mal's ovary was not behaving like a normal cyst, so they took out the ovary. They were sending it to pathology just in case.

Did someone tell our doctor she was overreacting when she took out the ovary? I like to picture her in the operating room, surrounded by colleagues, mostly men, saying *Leslie, it's nothing* and her saying *I hope for the patient's sake you're right but just in case*. She is old enough to have been one of the few women in her class. I wonder if that experience made her bolder or more cautious. Regardless, she caught the cancer before Mal had symptoms and probably she is the reason Mal is still alive.

The cancer diagnosis came two weeks later. The incisions were not yet healed and Mal still wasn't strong enough to carry her laptop in her shoulder bag. I spent another anxious morning in a waiting room while they dissected her lymph nodes and removed her other ovary. Her best friend and her mother fell into a comfortable rhythm of light conversation while I crossed my arms and stared at my laptop.

We met with the surgical oncologist. He told us the cancer had spread to one lymph node. Everything else was clear. This meant we had a good chance of surviving but we'd need to do half a year of highly toxic chemotherapy. That was the first time I said "we" in reference to Mal's diagnosis. For our whole relationship I'd fought hard against the "understood we" that couples often use. I felt it alienated single people and devalued other close relationships. I refused to say, "We liked that movie" or, "We don't eat meat," even when I made statements that applied to both of us. But from the first trip to the oncologist it was, "We have cancer."

In the parking lot Mal and I argued over who was driving home. In the car we fought about my being late and her being uptight about time. We hurled boring, predictable indictments at each other the way only two people who are deeply in love can: I never leave work early enough; she gives up too easily and doesn't challenge doctors enough. I stopped at a red light. She got out of the car and slammed the door behind her. I rolled my eyes, pulled over, and put on the hazard lights. I knew she'd come back and spend the rest of the day apologizing for bolting. I sat in the car recalibrating the next six months of our lives. Baldness. Puking. Fatigue. Doctor visits. Pain meds that don't work. Pain meds she throws up.

When she healed from the lymph node surgery we met the medical oncologist and his entourage of post-graduate not-quite-doctors who asked dumb questions like, *when was your last period?*

There was a new protocol for healthy women with ovarian cancer (yes, they say that), which involved delivering an especially toxic chemo drug directly to the abdominal cavity where the uterus and ovaries used to be. With a more concentrated drug the chance of getting all the microscopic cancer cells is greater. The chemo is administered through a port, which is surgically inserted. During the treatments Mal would have to lie on her side. Nurses would come in every twenty minutes to turn her over, like she was a rotisserie chicken. Some days they would give her the abdominal chemo and other days a more typical intravenous dose that would circulate around her body, they said, and kill microscopic cancer cells everywhere else.

What followed was months of Mal throwing up at three in the morning, and me calling the hospital, speaking to half-asleep residents who sounded so dismissive I could picture them rolling their eyes.

The problem with cancer—especially ovarian and breast—is that it forces you to be a woman. The first thing you see when you get off the elevator on the chemo floor is an advertisement for a program that teaches women how to apply makeup to hide the effects of cancer on their appearance. *Would they in a million years run a class like that for men?* I thought. *And what about carcinogenic chemicals in makeup?* At the other end of the hall was a store called Windows of Hope that sold pink and peach headscarves and long blonde wigs. We held hands tightly, and ridiculed forced femininity. It was as if our sarcasm about other women's choices about their gender presentations was the only thing keeping the ground under us.

Mal pulled her knit hat tight around her head, which had been shaved the night before by a friend who got kicked out of the military for being queer. He had called her "soldier" as he ran buzz clippers over her skull with a discipline and precision no civilian has.

It was an IV chemo day so Mal sat in a recliner in a large open room full of other people who looked too young to have cancer. Young women in pantsuits with pinstriped blouses didn't have brown rings around their eyes like Mal did. Maybe the makeup. Later we told the nurse how stupid we thought it was for the hospital to put so much emphasis on women's appearance. She told us how many of her patients were moms who were comforted by anything they could do to keep from looking so sick they scared their kids.

The chemo floor volunteers are sweet, gray-haired cancer survivors who offer you water and tell you how many years they've survived. They wheel snack carts right to the recliners so caregivers don't have to fetch ice chips and butter cookies. I liked having someone to take care of us. But I also needed to walk, and getting Mal ice chips gave me something to do. Moving my body kept me from getting too angry or scared. On my walks I often visited the Windows of Hope store. I ran my hands over the scarves because I needed to feel something soft.

Most of the snacks they gave us were Kraft or Nabisco, brands owned by the tobacco industry. I wondered how many people on the chemo floor had cancer because of the tobacco industry.

The cumulative effect of four months of chemo made Mal so sick she couldn't sleep or sit or stand. She called me at work crying. I sped home to drive her to the emergency room. They admitted her to the hospital that night so they could pump drug after drug into her veins, hoping something would stop the writhing. I called her best friend to meet us. But by morning Mal just wanted her mom. I believe in chosen family—they will come through for us when our genetic relatives, the people who rejected us when we came out, let us down. But Mal's parents didn't reject her. The narrative about the superiority of chosen family is mine alone. Still, I spent the next day in the hospital speaking to her mother in one-syllable grunts and I didn't thank her when she got me lunch. I gushed with gratitude over a friend who stopped by the hospital after work and stayed for half an hour.

I never expected to be a "marriage" gay. When I was young and single I poured as much time as I could into volunteering at an LGBTQ domestic violence organization. I distrusted couple-hood and only fell in love with people who didn't desire me. But meeting Mal made me trust more than I thought I could. We cried together at *Touched by an Angel*. We baked chocolate chip cookies and ate dough straight from the bowl. We wanted to sleep together every night so we outwaited my roommates and Mal moved in. I realized soon that I wanted to sleep with Mal every night for as long as I could imagine. We decided to have a ceremony in 2004, a month before the Goodridge decision made marriage legal in Massachusetts. *If one of us gets sick,* I explained to one of my more radical friends when she pressed me to justify our decision.

Being married gave me status. No nurse or ER doc or administrator could keep me from seeing her. A generation of activists had won victories that protected me from being removed from recovery rooms or not informed of test results. I was ready to get angry at any nurse or doctor or receptionist or phlebotomist who treated me as anything less than her next of kin. But since nobody did I had to get angry at cancer instead.

Mal's prognosis is so good because someone looked at the five-year survival rates for ovarian cancer and said, "This isn't acceptable." Someone was brave enough to risk ridicule when she or he asked a group of intelligent and accomplished colleagues, "What would happen if we delivered the chemo right into the abdominal cavity?"

I promise myself I will never be annoyed again by people who ask too many hard questions and are not satisfied by today's version of the best we can do. I also promise myself I will work hard at being a person whose teeth won't stop itching until we get to the next innovation. It's a promise I keep with varying degrees of conviction as the years of negative blood tests and normal pelvic exams add up.

I thought the minute Mal felt well enough to cook for herself I'd start supporting activist groups that fight environmental carcinogens, because what else would be logical when a person who is healthy and in her forties and negative for all the genetic tests gets sick? I was already an activist, a politicized consumer who bought fair trade and local when I could.

But instead we collect hats for the patients who now occupy the chemo recliners. We run races to raise money for ovarian cancer treatment. When I ask myself why, the only answer is this: We have fought the residents and the hospital and the disease and each other too much. We have exhausted our reserves of anger and we are too tired to fight. All we want now is hope and renewal. We are mobilized, but fragile. We choose the corporate-sponsored cancer love-fest for the same reason we choose a formulaic romantic comedy instead of a thought-provoking documentary. This, I fear, is why we will never get to the root cause of cancer.

B R Sanders

A Diagram of My Family

"Can you draw me a diagram?"

The words are as genuine as they are confused: my coworker has asked me to explain my family structure, cannot grasp it, and asks me to draw her a diagram.

"It's not that complicated," I tell her.

"I just don't get it. Maybe if I saw it."

"No, I don't think it would make more sense if you saw it."

Truly, my family isn't complicated. Jon, Samantha, and I live together and co-parent a wonderful rambunctious toddler named Zadie. One house, three adults, one child, two cats. Each of the three of us dates outside the family; I have a long-term, long-distance partner whom my kid calls Tia Hunter, and my partner Samantha has a boyfriend my kid has declared her best friend. Sure, we're queer. Sure, we're polyamorous. But if a family is a group of people, sometimes multigenerational, sometimes interracial, who love each other and support each other and who claim each other on their taxes, then we certainly count.

| | |

My kid, Zadie, is the heart of the family. She's our little sun, and we revolve around her: Mama, Daddy, and Baba. The whole Baba thing opens up a whole other can of worms when I mention it. A friend blinks in surprise. "You're Zadie's what now?"

"She calls me her baba."

"I thought you were her mother."

"No, Sam's her mom."

"But you had her, right? Like, I saw you, and you were pregnant."

"Well, yeah, but since I'm not a woman—"

"Oh, right you're gender..."

"Genderqueer. Trans*. Not a woman. Sam parents Zadie and is a woman, so she's the mama. And I parent her, and I'm nonbinary, so I'm the baba."

My friend gives me a skeptical look. "Alright. If you say so."

Again, a parenting nomenclature that is trans-inclusive does not seem so complicated or strange to me.

| | |

In my admittedly nontraditional family, I am the breadwinner. I am the only one of the three of us adults who has a standard, salaried position with health benefits. Because I am biologically related to my kid, I have never had a problem securing her health benefits. But I have been forced to choose between my partners, Samantha and Jon. Year after year I am forced to choose—which partner gets doctor's appointments? Meds? Covered urgent care? Jon has persistent foot problems, but Sam needs dental coverage.

We talked it over as a family. When I got this job, I married Jon so he could access my health care. Sam gave her blessing. At the time, she was still young enough to be partially covered by her father's benefits back home, but now she's aged out. Any time she has a cold or a toothache or takes a nasty fall on the ice I feel pangs of guilt. How is it possible that this wonderful person with whom I have forged a life, who stays at home and raises our kid—a much harder job than my cushy analyst position—is excluded from my benefits? Where is the sense in that? This is where my family turns from "complicated" to "not legally real." This is how confusion turns into injustice.

The irony of this is that while Jon and I are read as a straight couple (and certainly we have passing privilege—a fact that does not escape me when I am out with Samantha or my long-distance partner, Hunter) we are anything but. The State of Colorado sees a man and a woman wed in holy matrimony. In actuality, it's a man and a genderqueer who filed away a certificate and went on about their loving, consensually nonmonogamous, and decidedly queer partnership. Honestly, if Jon were to get a job that provided him health care tomorrow, I would divorce him and jump through all the ridiculous hurdles it would take to get Sam enrolled in my benefits.

I have no doubt that gay marriage is a meaningful and worthwhile pursuit for some people in the queer community. I am not one of them. I am more concerned with the equity my family currently lacks, the way the system has space for only two parents, and the fact that I can't get both of my spouses covered by my health insurance. I'm more concerned with the fact that I am an at-will employee who has to hide my gender identity for fear I'll be fired at work. Employment protections for trans* people are thin on the ground, and as the primary financial provider for my family and our single access point to employer-provided health care, I cannot afford to lose my job.

| | | |

To me, justice would look like a world where my family is not seen as complicated. For myself, I want a world that sees me for what I am and doesn't try to map me onto the ill-fitting gender binary. For my partners, I want a world that lets me care for them both equally. For Zadie, I want a world where she won't have to defend the legitimacy of her family to classmates and kids on the playground. I want society to see the breadth and inclusivity of my family the way I do: as the facts of my life, not as something as hollow and condescending as "lifestyle choices." For me and my family, marriage equality is the same old diagram drawn in pink instead of black. It's the same old word spoken with a slight accent. It will not help my nontraditional queer polyfamily get access to the resources and systems it needs. New words are gibberish to people who refuse to learn your language. Diagrams are useless to people who refuse to open their eyes.

Charles Rice-González

Shaping Bronx Queer Activism

I recall at a Gay Men of the Bronx general meeting late in 1992, one of our members, Ron Jacobowitz, a Jewish political activist whom we recognized as the founder of the group, asked to have a visitor added to our agenda. The visitor wanted to make a presentation and wanted GMoB to sign on to a flyer for a town hall meeting to discuss same-sex marriage. The young man was white, in his mid-twenties, and our group of about forty men assembled that day was about a quarter percent white and the rest primarily Black and Latino, a fair representation of the Bronx's demographics. He said that since Mayor Dinkins was poised to sign the executive order allowing domestic partnership registration in New York City, it would take our community to the next step, which would bring forth civil unions or same-sex marriage. His presentation was short and clear. After he finished, LaVenson Lockheart, a Black musician who was the facilitator at that meeting as it was the group's practice to rotate the facilitator, asked the group if we had any questions. The room blankly stared back at LaVenson and then Ron Jacobowitz prodded the group and asked if there was any discussion. The silence wasn't about disinterest; I felt the way many of the men felt—that it was an important issue, but not *the* important issue for us. Also, there was something fantastic about the idea of a man marrying a man or a woman marrying a woman, even at that time.

I realized that I wasn't interested in marriage. I wondered if it was because I never imagined it as a possibility, or because of the institutional weight it placed on defining what a relationship should be. And I knew my disinterest in gay marriage wasn't because I was afraid of commitment, because I had been in a relationship for about six years at that point and didn't feel like I needed the validation granted by being officially married by the state.

At the meeting, LaVenson looked around the room one last time, then held up our agenda. "I think we have a lot to discuss here." There was a general agreement with LaVenson. Ron, who had invited the guest, said that it was an important issue to which GMoB should be connected, so LaVenson asked the room if anyone opposed having GMoB's name on the flyer. I—along with the other men in the room—was eager to get on with our agenda. "I don't think we oppose, right?" Some guys shrugged, others nodded. "So, we are signing on?" The guys nodded and LaVenson said, "Okay, you can add us to the flyer. Next item." The young man thanked everyone and left.

The conversation after the young man left started with someone voicing, "I don't know what that has to do with us, given that I am a school teacher and I don't feel safe being found out, because I could lose my job." The conversation then sparked around the issue of gay marriage. But keeping in theme with the way the meetings were run, there was a general consensus that the issue was important, but the issues on our agenda were more pressing. In that particular meeting we talked a lot about safety, and there was a writer named Thomas Glave who talked about the fact that as men of color, most of us lived in neighborhoods that reflected us ethnically and that we didn't live in the West Village (*the* gay haven at that time). We talked about being out in our Bronx neighborhoods and how some of us wanted to blend into the urban look and fashion of our neighborhoods (thus the cocked baseball caps in the room), and we raised questions about where to live when we had partners, or for those of us with partners, how to navigate landlords and leases. These were the pressing issues that were affecting us at that moment in time. And AIDS was huge because many of our members had to leave the borough to get served. For example, the organization that brought meals to homebound people with AIDS, God's Love We Deliver, did not deliver to the Bronx back then.

We were still a nascent group but we were clear about what we wanted to do. We were clear about what we needed. So, we didn't need to be solely led by the groups meeting at the Lesbian and Gay Community Services Center on West Thirteenth Street or by the larger nonprofit organizations. We were creating our own agenda. We were looking at and shaping our lives as mostly working class and men of color, and voicing what was important to us.

Now we weren't alone in this activity of shaping our own queer lives. There was a group called BLUeS—Bronx Lesbians United in Sisterhood which had formed in 1989, a year before GMoB, that worked hand in hand with GMoB to change queer life in the Bronx through organizing our people, social events, political actions, advocacy, and sheer bravery. GMoB and BLUeS supported one another's efforts and found ways to work together. One campaign we did was to visit all of the local Bronx papers and ask them to include press releases and cover our events, actions, and activities. We needed to be seen in the Bronx. GMoB's mission included the phrases "combat isolation," "fight invisibility," and "create a supportive environment for gay men living and working in the Bronx." Although there had been Bronx-based queer groups before, GMoB and BLUeS lasted the longest (about ten years each) and they had the most lasting effect.

Historically, the center of queer activism was in Manhattan, but with the upsurge of AIDS, queer activism was rising in all of the city's five boroughs, and was also being taken on by cultural and ethnic groups like Gay Men of African Descent, Las Buenas Amigas, Weh Wah & Bar Che Ampe, P.R.I.D.E. (the Puerto Rican Initiative to Develop Empowerment), Latino Gay Men of New York, SALGA (South Asian Lesbian and Gay Association), GAPIMNY (Gay Asian Pacific Islander Men of NY) and AALUSC (African Ancestral Lesbians United for Societal Change). Being the sole voices from the Bronx, GMoB and BLUeS quickly rose to citywide recognition. Manhattan-based organizations saw the groups as conduits for local outreach and for collaborative work. Although GMoB toiled alongside many of the organizations like ACT UP, GMHC (Gay Men's Health Crisis) and AVP (The New York City Lesbian and Gay Anti-Violence Project), it was very much committed to the issues that were raised by its members at general meetings. Many new organizations emerged in Manhattan and many had white leaders who set the gay community's agenda by responding to issues they felt were at the fore of the concerns of gay New Yorkers. With GMoB and other groups coming into existence their agenda was becoming decentralized and diversified.

Being so close to the fire of change the downtown community was starting, we were conscious and eager to participate. There wasn't a void of leadership in the Bronx, so we could also express our own power. I don't know if we necessarily saw it that way, and it wasn't an "us versus them" mentality with the Manhattan groups: we were just organically in touch and aware of what we needed, and we understood that we had to be in the driver's seat for our own communities. We had to shape our reality. It was an exertion of power, because in some cases, like with LaVenson, who facilitated the meeting that night, his life literally depended on it. He had AIDS and Bronx AIDS Services (BAS) wasn't serving him: he wanted a support group for gay men who were HIV positive or who had AIDS, but the groups at BAS were focused on IV drug users who were primarily heterosexual. The data had not been collected on the number of gay people living with HIV and AIDS in the Bronx, so they didn't have funding for those groups. GMoB's Ron Jacobowitz, who also wanted an HIV-positive support group for gay men, started the group at BAS, and our gay brothers, like LaVenson, gathered there. So, BAS offered free meeting space and GMoB members led the group. Later, BAS received funding and took the group over and began programming geared toward gay men. Over ten years into the onset of AIDS, the Bronx's largest service organization had just begun to officially serve gay men.

But this recollection of that pivotal meeting where GMoB was asked to sign on to a same-sex marriage town hall sets the stage for how my living, working, and loving in the Bronx has been shaped. It gives a strong context to voicing what I feel is important in creating my life as a Black, Latino, working-class, educated gay man and artist from the Bronx. How do I navigate the balance between being connected to gay issues (like gay marriage) set by larger queer organizations that may or not be a priority in my life, and with other issues, concerns, and needs that hit home? How do I shape my life when I know there are other actions working at shaping my life? And both those activities are consistently coexisting.

I'm writing this at a moment when I can look back and see that the gay marriage agenda prevailed, and as far as New York is concerned, the legislation passed. The issue even reached the Supreme Court. And I can see how GMoB and later the Bronx had a role all along. Especially with the largest antigay marriage rally held in the Bronx and on the steps of the Bronx County Courthouse, organized by State Senator Reverend Ruben Díaz. I stood with about fifty Bronxites and another seventy-five people from citywide groups to hold our ground against thousands of church members who were bussed in from the tri-state area. We stayed involved in the gay marriage issue, but not at the risk of not addressing things that were important to our borough. Gay marriage prevailed, but so did serving LGBTQ people at BAS and other AIDS organizations that came later. Gay community centers came (and went), and the next one is in the works. The Bronx is persevering and preparing its third attempt at having a gay center, but looking at our history we can learn that other models haven't worked in the Bronx, and so we have to create a new one.

History shows that we were navigating how to live our lives, how to love and build relationships, how to live as gay men in the age of AIDS, and how to stay alive by not becoming HIV positive and/or learning to live as HIV-positive men. We were involved in creating the world in which we wanted to live, in shaping our reality, while knowing that there were (are) still factions and people in the world in which we lived who didn't want us to be alive. We were rising up—and not in a vacuum, because there were many groups forming all around New York City and all around the country—rising up because the totality of who we were as gay men living in the Bronx was not being addressed, and we didn't expect anyone else to speak to those concerns. Nobody would care about them in the way we did. Again, our lives and loves and how we lived them were at stake. We were chopping through the thicket of issues to create paths for ourselves, and later found that those paths were also cleared for others to follow.

We joined up with the rest of the country for the National March on Washington in 1993, but we also deepened our relationship at home with BLUeS. We spoke up alongside AVP (The New York City Lesbian and Gay Anti-Violence Project) and other groups at the Civilian Complaint Review Board when they put the homophobic Reverend Ruben Díaz on it, and we worked to build the first LGBTQ center in the Bronx, the Bronx Lavender Community Center. We marched in the Heritage of Pride Parade in Manhattan, but also marched in the Bronx Day Parade, and later worked to create our own gay pride events in the Bronx. We used our own creativity to develop resources so that we could do our work; one major way we did this was how GMoB pooled the creative resources of its members—several of whom had been or were drag queens, singers, musicians, dancers, actors—and created the fundraising event/variety show called Night of 12 Gowns, which ran for nearly ten years and raised the bulk of the money the organization needed to operate for the rest of the year.

The individual members of GMoB were also finding their own personal ways of creating the worlds in which we wanted to live. Adam Mark Kleinkopf formed a cable program called *Cornucopia Utopia* that broadcasted gay events on Bronx's public access television. Eric Booth followed suit with his own cable public access programming with *Strange Fruit*, a queer multicultural soap opera, and *Fruta Extraña*, a queer interview show. Jim O'Toole, a high school teacher at Walton High School, helped to advance one of the first queer student groups in the Bronx. Daniel DelValle continued developing his paintings and exhibited his work around town. Thomas Glave went on to publish several books, stories, and essays, some of which included stories about the Bronx. And in 1998, I teamed up with Arthur Aviles, an award-winning dancer and choreographer who came home to the Bronx to form his dance company after touring the world with the Bill T. Jones/Arnie Zane Dance Company, and formed BAAD! The Bronx Academy of Arts and Dance. And the members of GMoB came together to help the various initiatives. Many of the men helped produce Eric's *Strange Fruit* episodes, both in front of and behind the camera. Members of GMoB helped clean, hang lights, or did whatever was needed to help get BAAD! started, and now BAAD! celebrates fifteen years of being a queer space in the Bronx. Other men found partners, fell in love, made lifelong friends, and built circles of trust, love, friendship, and support. A social and cultural life had emerged in the Bronx, a life that was built on self-definition.

GMoB's actions to "combat invisibility and fight isolation to create a supportive environment for gay men who lived and worked in the Bronx" bore fruit, and those actions grew alongside many of the actions of the larger LGBTQ community while simultaneously finding individual expression.

I continue to shape my reality through my work with BAAD! and through writing. One thing I love about writing fiction—specifically fiction which features gay characters of color—is that it offers possibilities for how to live and love. I enjoy constructing worlds that are like the world we live in, and then placing characters in situations that they have to figure out. Perhaps the models that exist may not work for my characters, so they have to do something new, they have to shape their reality. I am very inspired by the Brecht quote that says, "Art is not a mirror held up to reality but a hammer with which to shape it."[i] With art and activism, I continue to shape my reality.

So, as a gay, working-class, Black, Latino man from the Bronx, I know that the road upon which I travel at times was paved by other people; at times its paths were being built as I drove toward them. Then, there were times when I needed to create the path myself in order to move forward. Standing in the year 2014 I see that GMoB and BLUeS did their jobs, but didn't develop in a way to continue forward. I can see a future where there won't be opposite-sex marriage and same-sex marriage, but simply marriage that will include all people. I know that the organizing around AIDS yielded great success: those affected now live full lives and manage the disease. I experience art by queer people (books, paintings, dance works, plays, etc.) that continues to shape the world and create possibilities exemplified by what have become classic works like *The Normal Heart*, having a successful award-winning revival on Broadway and on cable television, and at the same time BAAD!'s gay, Latino holiday play, *Los Nutcrackers: A Christmas Carajo* has been produced and presented to sold-out audiences for the past decade. And those efforts helped pave the way for transgender artists, like Laverne Cox and Roman Rimer, to create art that brings audiences into their experiences.

Being out and organizing in the Bronx has taught me to carve my own way in a world that often has different priorities, like gay marriage, which was embraced by my larger queer community. I have hope that one of the great things that gay couples can bring to marriage is the experience and knowledge of how to be creative in constructing our relationships. That while there may be paths built by others, many of us, in the Bronx and beyond, will be defining how we love, how we build our lives, and how we shape our queer realities.

Notes

[i] Paulo Freire, A Critical Encounter, ed. Peter McLaren and Peter Leonard, (London, New York: Routledge, 2004), 79.

Jackson Shultz and Kristopher Shultz

It's Complicated

A Trans Perspective on the Marriage Debate

In 2009, amidst a flurry of protesting and counter-protesting, flag waving and petitioning, hatemongering and gay-agendizing, my partner and I held a domestic partnership ceremony in the big city of Waitsburg, Washington. Locally known as "that place where Highway 12 curves," Waitsburg is probably the last place where anyone could imagine a rather large queer ceremony would occur. Yet, on a sunny August morning around one hundred guests filtered into the rows of chairs we had arranged in Mrs. Wilson's pasture. The cows stuck their heads over the fence, watching placidly as my partner and I strolled down the aisle hand in hand, our mothers on our arms. As we neared the front of the pasture, our guests ceased speculating on the gender of our ring bearer and smiled up at us encouragingly.

Our ceremony officiator, a butch Chicana clad in a scout's uniform and rainbow neckerchief, lectured us on the importance of being positive role models in our relationship. She reminded us that as queerfolk we don't often have positive examples of how a same-sex relationship dynamic might work: many of our queer elders struggle to find balance in their own relationships, and many more are too closeted in their personal affairs to be willing to provide guidance to younger generations. She then directed her lecture to the audience, reminding them that as young queers, and especially as two transgender individuals, my partner and I would need as much support as we could get. As our friends and family, she advised, our ceremony attendees should be prepared to support us in whatever ways they could. While a few present were taken aback by the request of a woman sporting an "I went on a beaver sleepover" badge, most have gone out of their way to show my partner and me unending support.

Although our ceremony had some traditional wedding aspects (because, let's face it, everyone wants to catch a rainbow garter), we were conscious in our planning and our recognition that we were not getting married. Our service was held while same-sex marriage opponents were collecting signatures to get Referendum 71 on the ballot, in an effort to overturn Washington's everything-but-marriage domestic partnership expansion. We actively wanted a domestic partnership rather than a marriage, and until the 2012 elections we were content with this arrangement.

The January prior to our ceremony, my partner had been hospitalized with undiagnosed abdominal pain. The physicians were less than thrilled with my presence and asked me to leave the room on a number of occasions. Since my partner and I both present as male, we are first faced with homophobia in medical situations, followed by transphobia once one of us discloses our trans identity. My partner was not conscious enough to make his own medical decisions, yet he was trapped in a vulnerable state, alone with doctors who asked him inappropriate questions about his genitalia, completely unrelated to any of his symptoms. When I was in the hospital room, the surgeon said such asinine things as, "If I press on your ovaries, do you feel pain in your testicles? Oh wait, *you* don't have testicles." I cannot imagine, and my partner cannot remember, what terrible comments were made when I was *not* there to advocate for him.

I've lost count of the number of times a physician or nurse has asked me the last date of my menstrual cycle and stared expectantly at me until I finally sigh incredulously and tell them "2008." As trans folk, navigating the medical system is complicated enough without the compounding factor of homophobia. Our negative experiences at the hospital spurred us to register as domestic partners, despite the fact that we were still undergraduates. Had we not needed the semblance of legal protection that registering as domestic partners afforded us, we likely would have waited until we had minimally completed our degrees before we made a legal commitment to one another.

Imperfect timing aside, we were extremely thankful that we had registered as domestic partners in August when I developed a kidney infection the following November. When we arrived at the emergency room, my partner was asked to show his domestic partnership card before he was allowed to enter my room. In similar situations, my sister and her husband have never once been asked to produce their marriage certificate to prove the validity or preexistence of their union. Such was the culture of eastern Washington that we always kept our cards on our person in case of emergencies. Out of habit, or perhaps to keep my gym membership card company during its frequent months of disuse, I still keep my domestic partnership card in my wallet to brandish about whenever a discriminatory moment should present itself.

Most recently, my partner and I had the pleasure of presenting our domestic partnership card to a befuddled waitress. We were at a restaurant and ordered a bottle of wine. The waitress requested our IDs and promptly asked if we were brothers. We laughed a bit and told her that we were not, in fact, brothers. She handed our IDs back and said we'd need to order something else. Perplexed, we asked her why, and she responded triumphantly at her cunning ability to catch us lowly scam artists in the act: "You have the same last name and the same address, but you're not brothers."

There was a certain amount of facepalming before my partner had the presence of mind to pull out our domestic partnership card and explain to her that there might be more than one reason that two dudes would share a last name and address. She was incredibly apologetic and had the grace to comp our drinks. This was not the first confusion caused by our last names nor, I'm sure, will it be the last.

My partner and I are frequently asked which one of us changed our last name, why we changed, and how we can live with ourselves for following a practice that is so unfeminist. When my partner turned eighteen, he changed his first name to something more suited to his transmasculine identity, and he changed his last name to his mother's maiden name, thus removing the patriarchal influence of his divorcé father. I did not take his name to insinuate that I am submissive in the relationship, that I am property, or that I support traditional gender roles. I took his last name because I grew up in a blended family, and I spent an equal number of years living with my father and with my stepfather, both of whom are wonderful parents and role models. As they both had an equal hand in raising me, I felt that sharing one of their last names was a disservice to the other, and I jumped at the chance to take the last name my partner chose for himself.

While many of my feminist-minded friends scoff that I would change my name at all, I like that our mail comes to Mr. and Mr. Shultz. While we know in queer communities that sharing a common surname has nothing to do with being family, our last name is nevertheless a sign to the rest of the world that we are somehow related. As demonstrated by the overly ambitious alcohol-screening waitress, we are frequently mistaken for brothers or cousins. Whenever a misunderstanding such as this occurs, we decide whether or not it is safe or viable to explain to the offending TSA officer, waitress, or cashier who questioned our relationship doubted that we're in a long-term, fairly monogamous, financially committed, everything-but-marriage domestic partnership.

Despite what our shared surname seems to imply, we remain defiantly unmarried, because we feel that our relationship is about so much more than marriage, and we have found that marriage doesn't necessarily add any value to the way we feel about each other. We refer to one another as "partner" rather than "spouse." We occasionally throw in a nickname spawned from the headlines around Washington's domestic partnership expansion when someone uses the H-word. I find myself saying, "Why, yes, my everything-but-husband *is* an excellent cook," or, "No, my everything-but-spouse isn't home right now, may I take a message?"

Somehow, others don't seem to find this nearly as amusing as I do. Those who believe I support marriage equality assume I'm implying that the domestic partnership laws in Washington are not good enough. Those who believe I do not support marriage equality assume I am attempting to affirm my position against marriage, never minding that I'm in a domestic partnership. Given that my stance on marriage equality has changed over the years, I can hardly blame their confusion. At times like these, I do very little to confirm or deny their suspicions: I find that being enigmatic is necessary to my survival as a trans person.

When I was new to LGBTQ organizing and activism, I remember handing out leaflets on my college campus in support of marriage equality. I distinctly recall parroting such phrases as, "Separate but equal does not work!" and "Civil unions are second class!" It took me several years to realize that marriage was the least of my concerns. While my initial activism was based around such mainstream goals as marriage equality, military inclusion, and finding a good sale on designer ascots—over time, I found myself distracted. Somewhere in between having to quit my job when I came out as trans, being the survivor of a shockingly well-publicized hate crime, and attempting to finish school without a scholarship that was apparently predicated on my remaining a woman, my passion for marriage equality was shunted to the back burner.

I'm certain I'm breaking the Ten Gay Commandments blaspheming like this, but marriage equality is not high on my list of priorities for LGBTQ communities. The amount of time, money, and resources that have been used to further the goal of marriage equality could have been put to better use combating LGBTQ homelessness; working toward a cure for HIV/AIDS; providing safe-sex education for queer youth; pushing for antidiscrimination policies that are trans-inclusive; developing tighter bonds with intersex communities; and fighting racism, ableism, and classism within our communities. As trans folk our communities continue to be plagued by the realities of murder, sexual assault, violence, and discrimination. Our preoccupation with issues of immediate survival means we don't have time to wait for the implied trickle-down benefits that marriage equality promises in terms of investments, taxes, or estate rights. Furthermore, the need for protections like property benefits implies that one has been able to find work, establish savings, and purchase property. Many trans folk, facing overt forms of discrimination, cannot find housing protections to rent an apartment, let alone find and keep work that would afford them the resources needed to buy a home.

Marriage as we know it comes with a set of social rules and pressures that don't conform to, or even coincide with, the ways in which many queer relationships function. I have yet to meet the polyamorous or queer atheist individual who feels that marriage equality is an institution in which they are eager to take part. The current lack of separation between a civil marriage and a religious marriage is immensely troubling, and it is hard to imagine a relationship model that is further from the dynamic I have witnessed in the majority of my LGBTQ friends. Marriage equality seems to be as divisive an issue as deciding which of the *Queer Eye* guys would look best in leather: it's a friendship-ending conversation that we can't seem to escape.

Why we cannot reimagine marriage as something other than a simultaneously religious and civil union of only two people is beyond me. LGBTQ communities are pushing to take part in a practice that has a horribly low success rate, without pausing to realize that we have an incredible opportunity to push for a completely different option. We could grant legal protections for those who need them, allow religious ceremonies for those who want them, and celebrate our love without being forced into the narrow concept of what constitutes a "legitimate" marriage. By failing to recognize our collective power to dismantle the current civil/religious marriage dichotomy, we are ignoring our radical queer potential, which is a disgrace and a dishonor to our queer foremothers, forefathers, and fore-non-binary parental units who often fought to dismantle patriarchal systems such as marriage.

My partner and I both fully agree that our relationship is about so much more than marriage, yet we understand the push for greater safety and acceptance. With the passing of Washington's new marriage equality bill, we are faced with a difficult decision. On June 30, 2014, all same-sex domestic partnerships will be converted to marriages if no action is taken. Do we simply let our partnership become a marriage, despite the fact that marriage isn't an institution that we support or one to which we consented? Do we file to dissolve our domestic partnership and risk the loss of rights such as hospital visitation, the ability to file taxes jointly, guardianship protections should we have a child, and all manner of property and estate provisions? Do we dissolve our partnership and try to find a state with non-marriage protections for same-sex couples, and if so, how long will it be before we're forced to convert to marriage or abandon our partnership in that state?

Our stance on marriage is paradoxical: as transgender individuals, we believe that marriage is the wrong goal and that we need to focus on the most vulnerable and marginalized portions of our communities, yet precisely because we are transgender, we need the protections that marriage provides—more so than most gender-conforming couples. Marriage is not an institution in which we wish to participate, but we cannot ignore the fact that we have grown used to the protections afforded us by our domestic partnership. Is it honestly too much to ask that we continue to receive these basic legal rights and responsibilities without having to participate in a religious practice in which neither of us believe?

We have yet to reach a decision regarding whether or not we will dissolve our domestic partnership prior to June. We know that marriage is a high priority for many within our communities, but as trans folk we continue to be frustrated by the sheer amount of time and resources that have been funneled into the marriage equality movement, while the issues and needs of the most marginalized members of our communities continue to be neglected. Within most LGBTQ spaces our opinion on marriage is highly unpopular, and because our communities are so small and fractionalized, we do our best to keep our divisive opinions to ourselves while we figure out what we're going to do about our own partnership. In the end, it may come to a coin toss between standing by our principles and needing to protect ourselves in the event of a medical or legal emergency. In the meantime, my everything-but-husband and I will privately continue our discussions on marriage, domestic partnerships, and of course, which *Queer Eye* guy would look best as a leather daddy.

A.M. O'Malley

The Empire Builder

The westbound train, *Empire Builder*, departs Chicago's Union Station in the early afternoon; the bustling station waves goodbye to the train as she travels north to Milwaukee. The train passes through the verdant rural landscape of Wisconsin, crossing the Upper Mississippi River at La Crosse. She travels through southeastern Minnesota, crosses the Mississippi again, and stops in Saint Paul. Then, the land changes from forest to prairie, becoming less populous and more barren. Westbound passengers see only the occasional mercury-vapor light of farmsteads in the distance. As the *Empire Builder* passes through North Dakota, near-ghost towns can be seen.

Eventually, the train gets past the prairies of North Dakota and Montana, with three short stops near Glacier National Park, followed by a longer stop in Whitefish, Montana. Mountain vistas can be seen from the observation car as it skirts the edge of the park. As darkness descends again, the train continues through the mountains, including northern Idaho and eastern Washington. In Spokane, the train splits, like a broken tooth, with half going down the Columbia River valley to Portland, Oregon, and the other half through the Cascades to Seattle, Washington.

It was November in Minneapolis when I left, a particularly gray and cold year. The hedges around the neighbor's yard were still crying red from autumn's song, though, and I missed them even before I had packed my last bag. I missed everything before I left: I missed the loud-mouthed kids in Powderhorn Park, I missed the May Day Cafe's broccoli quiche, I missed the sure promise of crunching snow and snapping cold. Mostly, I missed Avi and Ariel, my chosen family, and the house we called Dogwood Cabin. I missed the hours we sat there, around Avi's oak table, talking about love, music, books, and everything else. I missed the smells of tobacco smoke, wet dog fur, and coffee that permeated the cabin. I missed the clamoring dogs, skulking cats, and drafty windows of south Minneapolis.

I had decided to ride west in the low belly of the *Empire Builder*, the longest possible route. I rode west for love, for Amy—a reason that felt more important than anything at the time. I was riding to start my own family, a queer family. I was leaving behind my Midwestern roots, I was leaving behind blood relations who didn't understand my queerness. I wanted to start over, start new. I was taking a geographical cure for feeling "other than," for not being in a "real family."

I envisioned a ride of reflection and long journal entries; Avi had taught me solitaire games for the trip. I boarded late in the night, at the small station in Saint Paul. I went alone to the train station, loaded my boxed bicycle and three giant duffel bags, everything I had left. I bought a one-way ticket, feeling giddy at the thought. One way, no looking back. I tried to stop missing what I was leaving behind as I sat in the station waiting to board. I tried not to think about my grandfather, who I surely wouldn't see alive again, tried not to think of what I was rejecting, and tried to think of what lay ahead.

The night before I left, Avi made curry. The aged, former crusty-punk, queer family that I'd been enveloped in during the years I lived in South Minneapolis was all around Avi's oak table. I took one bite of the spicy curry and burst into tears. We all cried, and then we all laughed, and then we rode our bikes through the night to sing karaoke. After that, I tried to stop missing; I looked forward.

I packed, threw out, or gave away everything I had accumulated in Minneapolis: dumpstered shelves, a beautiful Formica kitchen table, a curving couch found at a garage sale, even my 1940s-era Kitchen Aide mixer had to go—it was too fragile.

My mom pronounces Oregon as "Oree-gone," and as I was packing my things and saying my goodbyes, she asked over and over if I had a rain jacket. "It rains there three hundred days of the year," she said, sitting on my bed as I packed boxes of books for her to store in her chicken coop. I reassured her that I had all the gear I needed. The look on her face told me that she knew I felt I had to leave in order to be free to start a family with Amy, but we didn't talk about it. Before she left, with boxes piled high in her truck, my mom whispered that she loved me, as if it were a secret.

I was going west for Amy—young and vigorous, and madly in love with me. I wanted what she felt; I wanted that feeling of devotion. She had gone back to Portland before me; she was sleeping in the attic of her parents' house, writing me long love letters and making devotional mixtapes. We had worked ourselves into a frenzy of missing, until I, in the fever of love, quit my waitressing job, told my five roommates I was leaving, and called my mother to ask for a small loan to cover my train ticket. It had all happened quickly, three weeks between decision and departure. Amy was offering what I had always wanted someone to be as my person—my partner—and I was willing to dive into the unknown for that sense of belonging.

The train rocked back and forth on its finite lines. That first night I just sat in the dark and counted the minutes as miles, thought about the hours it would take to get me there, to Portland. I had brought along the saddest words of Joan Didion: *The Year of Magical Thinking*, a story of loss so deep that it came through to another side of living, as if grief were a sword. She lost her husband—and almost her daughter—in the same year. I felt pulled apart by her words; there on the train, riding west, I felt that loss. I felt the loss of the familiar, of the people who were my queer family, and of my blood family, too. Unlike her, I was still holding on to a safe bet: the bet that Amy was waiting for me at that far away train station.

I rode west in the belly of the slow-moving *Empire Builder*, fifty miles an hour, across nineteen hundred miles. I had plenty of time to ponder how many thousands had started over on this exact route. How many thousands had pegged their futures on Oregon, on the West? These thoughts kept me company as I watched the landscape slowly change outside my window. The scenery grew more and more alien, no longer the gray Minneapolis fall, and I felt a surge of sudden skin-freezing panic, four hundred miles into the trip. I was caught in a place between places. My beautiful reasons flickered and faltered momentarily. I went to the back of the train and willed it backwards; it pushed onward.

Grey turned to brown. North Dakota's low, rolling Turtle Mountains passed in the night. Montana spread herself for the probing *Empire Builder*. Brown gave way to glacier. The glass in the observation deck was coated in grime and expectation; I waited to see the shrugging shoulders of the Cascades.

I tried to sleep. The young man next to me had impossibly shiny shoes for such a long journey. I watched him in the semidarkness that second night; we were so close without touching. The only thing protecting us from the November elements were the steel walls of the *Empire Builder*. The young man with shiny shoes and I lay side by side. He snored softly with his mouth agape, looking fragile in the thin reading light that I poured down on him.

The route took us through thirty-six hours of mountains and flatlands. I spent the last hours of the journey in a booth on the observation deck, plugged into the mixtape that Amy had made for me, watching the earth change. Glacier turned into mist and blackberry brambles, and the air became visible with rain.

In the late morning, the train rode into what looked like a Gus Van Sant movie, and the young man with shiny shoes went with half the train to Seattle; we never spoke. The rain had washed away the grime on the observation car, but the expectation was still there. I was home, for the first time. I was ready for this.

The Gus Van Sant movie gave way to Humphrey Bogart and Lauren Bacall—*To Have and Have Not*, 1944: The air is misty and Lauren waits for Humphrey on a dirty train platform. Her honey hair is wrapped in a fetching scarf, eyes welling with tragedy. They kiss in that slightly rough way of '40s films, and he leaves her standing there. I kept my face pressed to the glass while my mixtape blared.

Amtrak doesn't allow for romantic waiting on train platforms anymore, so when I stepped off the train, it was to luggage handlers shouting to each other and weary passengers pushing past me.

Amy was waiting just inside the door, leaning forward on a counter, watching me approach—her hand covering her mouth, her eyes unreadable. I stopped in front of her and dropped my bag. We stood like that for hours—or maybe just a few minutes—both waiting, poised, for the other, for our new family.

Regina Sewell

Unequal Wedding

My wife, Jenna, and I got married last September, and even though our ceremony was legally recognized, we do not feel equal. After years of being denied the right to marry, it was hard to trust that our marriage would actually count, even though we live in a state where same-sex marriage is legal. In fact, until we got our marriage license in the mail, part of me was afraid that our application would be denied. It was irrational, but I expected to get a letter from the town court explaining that since we had not filled out a form that was impossible to find or had not jumped through a hoop that we didn't know about, our wedding was invalid.

In the end, the Supreme Court's ruling on DOMA ensured that our marriage is legal at the federal level so that my wife and I are entitled to all the benefits other married couples get. But changes in the law don't translate into changes in other people's attitudes and they don't counteract a lifelong sense of feeling flawed. Getting married brought both of these issues front and center.

We knew that her parents would be uncomfortable with the news and weren't sure that they would be able to support our marriage. They are very Catholic and even though they like me—maybe even love me—in their mind, our relationship is a sin. We broke the news to them in person, framing our decision to get married through the lens of insurance benefits. It felt more like an apology than an announcement. Jenna told her father that because of Obamacare, I would have to get insurance and pointed out that it would be much cheaper for me if we got married. He ranted about Obama and the Affordable Care Act. And then we ate, as if nothing had happened.

It was even harder to tell my parents. They love Jenna. They ask about her every time I talk to them. In their minds, Jenna and I are a pair. But my family has always lived by a "Don't Ask, Don't Tell" policy. They tacitly agree to be gracious and welcoming to Jenna, and we reciprocate by not making them acknowledge that we are a couple. On top of this, my mother has Alzheimer's, and it is simply too much for her tangled brain cells to grasp that I have a female partner.

Ultimately, I never told my mother about the wedding. She still doesn't know that I got married. I told my father as an aside. I called him to ask if he had my birth certificate. When he asked why I needed it, I told him that I was getting married. I don't think he knew what to say so I explained that by getting married, I could get insurance.

His reaction came the next day, via email. He said that he was glad that I was going to have insurance and wished us luck. But he also asked me not to announce my wedding to the rest of his family. Even though I had no intention of doing so, the fact that he asked me not to hurt. He was ashamed and didn't want his family to know his daughter was queer.

As for the ceremony, getting married is a big deal and we wanted it to be a celebration. We wanted to be surrounded by people who loved us, who were happy for us and could easily support our union. Our parents couldn't do this so we didn't invite them. And since we weren't inviting our parents, it seemed awkward to invite other relatives. In the end, we only invited a few very close friends. We had a beautiful ceremony with fabulous music, but it would have been nice had our parents been there, embracing us and supporting our union.

At the time, we barely acknowledged how much our parents' lukewarm support hurt us. We both grew up understanding that there was something intrinsically wrong with being gay, so we never expected our parents to love us unconditionally. We learned to be grateful for the love they could give us, even more grateful because they could love us even though we were "defective." As a consequence, when we got married, we were more concerned about our parents' shame and discomfort than how devastating it felt knowing that our love made them uncomfortable and ashamed.

Instead, we felt flawed. Here we were, disappointing our parents yet again. And by planning a wedding they would not be asked to witness, we took on their shame. And acknowledging that we felt flawed, that we felt like disappointments, that we took on their shame, required us to acknowledge that we betrayed ourselves. We sold out our dignity for conditional love.

It's not just our families' reactions that we had to face. Getting married required us to "come out" to strangers, and it was scary. You don't have to tune into the Rush Limbaugh Show or watch footage of Fred Phelps and his Westboro Baptist Church flock waving signs that say "God Hates Fags" to know that there are people out there who hate us. The message is on the daily news.

Besides, both of us have been rejected, called names, and felt misunderstood because we are queer. We've learned to brace ourselves for other people's disapproval and rejection.

In order to get married, we had to fill out an application with a town clerk. Even though New York is a relatively gay-friendly state, dread mixed with excitement as we sat in the parking lot outside town hall preparing to go in. We didn't know if we'd be welcomed or treated like scum. We felt the same dread when we had to contact the insurance representatives to make sure we were both on the policy, and when we went to the bank to update our accounts. The dread escalated to full-blown fear when there was an incident in the neighborhood and we had to talk to the police as wives.

And even though, so far, the responses have been professional, we still end up feeling like second-class citizens because we have to be prepared for possible negative reactions. And there are still lots of places where we don't feel comfortable going and places where we are afraid to hold hands in public lest we get bashed. The hyper-vigilance is exhausting.

So, I've walked down the aisle. I'm married to the love of my life. And in the eyes of the Internal Revenue Service, my marriage is the same as a heterosexual marriage. But I still feel that same shame, fear, guilt, and uncertainty because I'm queer. The laws denying same-sex relationships may soon be history, but the hatred and prejudice that enacted those laws linger on. And that hatred has burned scars deep into my soul. I know that my wife and I are not the only ones who feel them. If we want to truly achieve equality, we have to heal these scars and change the culture that causes them. Ironically, one of the most powerful ways we can do this is by getting married. Getting married is the new coming out. It challenges us to face our scars, pushes those close to us to explore their homophobic attitudes, and normalizes our relationships to the world at large.

Everett Maroon

In a Small Town, Nothing Goes Wrong

Preamble

Walla Walla is the definition of small town, so much so that the chamber of commerce petitions its candidacy for every contest looking to name the next "best small town." With two blocks of lively downtown shopping, beat cops who know the townsfolk by name, and country doctors who've taken care of families from grandmother to granddaughter, there are many people here who insist that Walla Walla is a near utopia. The city is much more in beat with the Old West than the Pacific Northwest, which I discovered when I moved here from the East Coast. I made the left turn at Spokane on the homestretch of a weeklong drive, and gasped. For one, the topography between the Cascade Mountains and the Rockies is all scrubland. There's not a conifer anywhere along the three-hour drive from Spokane to Walla Walla that some intrepid soul didn't plant there. While the Washington license plates boast that this is the Evergreen State, Walla Walla births armies of new gray-brown tumbleweeds every winter in defiance. The Blue Mountains just to the east of the city may boast trees two stories high, but in the valley, where the city sits, there are only pothole-strewn streets and the trees planted at the turn of the last century, trees that are falling over one by one when a powerful storm front moves through.

Nearly every conversation I had with city residents when we first ambled into town—our eyes unbelieving at the massive brick houses, the roads lined with churches of all stripes and building design, the maximum security penitentiary and its thick razor wire fences next to the highway—included some version of the "Walla Walla is a great place to live" mantra. Sometimes this sentiment revolved around family, as in "Walla Walla is a great place to raise kids." The first dozen times it was said to me I nodded, still adjusting to the move after living in Washington, DC for a decade. But then I felt the need to push back. When confronted with a "but you know your neighbors here," I would counter with "I knew my neighbors in DC, too." In truth the lack of traffic and commuting is laudable, but the deficiencies are strewn about like the acorns squirrels—who are not native to this area—leave around in city parks.

Walla Walla's two hospitals are better prepared to airlift a gravely injured person 225 miles over the mountains to Seattle than to treat them here. Our high school hasn't had an infrastructure upgrade for twenty-five years. The businesses doing well on Main Street are bordered by two blocks at the east and west ends of downtown that haven't had tenants since the 2008 recession, their faded clearance and "we're closing" signs a desperate testimony to the lethargy of economic revival here in the valley. We have no child psychiatrist, no HIV specialist, no homeless shelter for teens, no anti-bullying campaigns, and no LGBTQ advocacy organization. There's no clear answer as to their absence; maybe the city council doesn't prioritize such things, or maybe having such resources goes against the idea of Walla Walla's municipal perfection.

Because if we worked to pass a bond and fix the high school building, we'd in some way admit that it had significant structural failures. If we brought in a child psychiatrist, we'd have to acknowledge that some of our children have problems larger than what a few hugs and an afternoon at Camp Fire can fix. Instead, we've collectively opted to look in a different direction and congratulate ourselves for our successes. We've opted to count our love of community by the number of free hot dogs handed out on National Night Out for Safety instead of how many free breakfasts our schools serve to our youngest students.

It's this willingness to ignore whole groups of people and problems that defines the framework for local LGBTQ activism. Back in 1990 when I became involved in the LGBTQ community at the ripe old age of twenty, marriage for queer people wasn't anything I thought would happen in my lifetime. I was okay with that. As a queer person I, like others, had learned to value relationships through community connections with other LGBTQ people, and through a constant reinforcement that it was us against the conservative culture-makers who despised us. Polyamorous relationships, serial monogamy, people who held informal or made-up ceremonies to express their commitment to each other—all of these were considered equally valid paths for intimacy among adults. With no state legitimatization of LGBTQ relationships, we were left to our own imaginations and companionship arrangements. Now that the state's vision of marriage has been the goal of so much LGBTQ money and energy (approximately $30 million was spent in the 2012 pro-marriage campaigns in Washington, Maine, and Maryland)[i], we've pushed aside our hard-fought diversity of relationship structures, and in that act of disrespect, we've lost sight of the queer and trans people who don't have marriage as their priority. For many of us in the LGBTQ spectrum, especially we rural folk who have far fewer resources available to us, I can think of some other issues that ought to be at the forefront of a political movement. Namely:

1. Youth: He's so much tinier than I imagined, with tendril-like fingers and a neck so slender I marvel that it's large enough for all the tubes, muscles, and bones the human body demands in that area of the body. Maybe I've somehow wound up in Lilliput, because I feel like a giant in comparison to him—the orc and the elf sitting in a coffee shop to talk about being transgender in our little city. I try to put aside my ridiculous thought process and focus on the point of our conversation. I'm the first live trans person he's met since telling his parents more than two years ago that he wanted to live as a boy. He's fifteen and I'm forty-three, and this gap makes me concerned about how we look to passersby.

He should be a second-year high school student. Instead he's taking classes at the community college. A scant few months ago he was an honor roll student at Walla Walla High School, but that was before he sat in the principal's office with his mother and revealed he'd be transitioning and using a new name. That was before the principal, known for being a sensitive guy, told the student he didn't think he could protect him from bullying and suggested he leave the public school—the only mainstream high school in town. For this teenager, it's not the leaky roof or makeshift classroom trailers hitched together around the grounds of the school that are a distraction to learning, it's the entire school. He tells me in quiet sentences about his situation, said matter-of-factly even as he explains there are no other options for him. I keep nodding, trying to hide any expression, fiddling with my now-cooled mug.

Not everybody is on a college trajectory, and certainly not everybody wants to be. But this kid saw education as his passport out of Walla Walla, and now he'll get a GED, which will limit him.

Colleges expect a high school diploma after four years of work. I talk to Masen Davis, director of the Transgender Law Center in San Francisco, when he comes to town to give a lecture, and ask about strategies to support the student. I send out a blind-copy email message to see if I can cobble together a group to put pressure on the school board. Could we get them to change their stance on trans kids in school? Offer this student a high school diploma for his course work at the community college? Get them to commit themselves to some cultural competency training? Even these remedial allowances are likely to be met with resistance, but I'm a patient trans man. Months later I meet a senior staff member from the superintendent's office who tells me the principal is hiring a trainer to educate all of the faculty and administration on trans issues. And then they plan to hold a mandatory meeting with the students. It's good news, even if it comes a bit late.

My inbox beeps and I read that there's another transmasculine student who lives in the labor camp on the outskirts of town. He's the child of migrant farmers—Washington State invites 80,000–120,000 foreign farm laborers to pick fruit every year—who work long days on either side of daylight, except for when they head to Mass at the Spanish-speaking Catholic church on Alder Street. It's one of the few structures in Walla Walla that pops out as part of the skyline, standing above the low buildings that huddle together in the valley. His folks have just kicked him out, having discovered that he identifies as male. Being sixteen and homeless and trans and Latino and poor—I put those statuses together and feel an overwhelming sense of urgency. There is no teen shelter in town, and no sense among local child protective services staff that in a recent national study, 40 percent of teens seeking shelter were LGBTQ-identified.[ii]

I make a few calls around town: Will alerting child services wind up getting his parents deported? Should the goal be to get him back in his home, even if his parents don't accept him? Is it ethical for me to identify the resources in town if I don't know his specific preferences? My link to him—my other trans teen friend's mother—tells me his aunt said she will take him in for the night, but can't house him long term. She confirms that the parents are primarily concerned with what their community and their priest will think; they presume they're failures as parents, and now their child is irredeemably lost.

I drive over to the Catholic church with my toddler in tow, because somehow he makes me braver, and I find the padre, a man who has a wrestler's body and an ever-present smile. I've heard that he's been key in breaking up gang fights in town and getting juveniles out of the gang system. He and I both have those stupid Transitions lenses that are sensitive to the sun—the sun is almost always shining here. As we stand outside in our temporary sunglasses, with our dark hair and olive skin, I reckon we look like wannabe mafiosi, even if neither of us is Italian. I ask him if he would talk to the parents, or at least deliver a sermon on Sunday about loving your family and not judging them. He agrees to both, but in the meantime the teen's uncle convinces the parents to take him back in, so for now, he has a home.

It will be eighteen months until the teen becomes a legal adult, and in many ways that is not a boon for him. I try to imagine the padre standing at the microphone in church the next Sunday, the light filtering through stained glass windows, a crucified Jesus hanging behind him, reminding parents that their love for their children is a tiny slice from the divine, or that it is God's will that they offer their children unconditional support. But I don't go to Mass anymore. I just hope that the parents in the room take his words as the permission to love that he intends it to be.

In Walla Walla, there are plans for a teen shelter, but they've been stuck in the planning stages for a few years now, and nobody on the planning board has taken the specific needs of LGBTQ adolescents into account in any part of their process. We pretend that it's the perils of adolescence and rebellion, not systemic oppression for gender nonconforming and queer kids. Two boys under twenty-one have committed suicide in town in the last five years to a mild degree of attention that quickly faded, but nobody has muttered a syllable about gay or queer or trans, even as folks litter their relatives' Facebook pages with pictures of teddy bears and crosses.

2. Political Advocacy: In any given week, I get contacted by a counselor, acquaintance, or friend of a friend looking to see if there are any adult transgender support groups in the city (there aren't), any good books trans youth should read, or any legal advocates who could help with a particular situation. In September a trans woman on one of the Valley Transit busses—they are designed to look like quaint trolleys—was openly mocked by the driver, who outed her status to the other passengers. She got off four stops before her destination, afraid for her safety. Her friend who knows me asked if I could sit down for a meeting and give the harassed woman any advice. With no clause for "gender identity or expression" in the city's antidiscrimination law, she would have had more recourse for being mocked as a cis woman. I message her on Facebook to say I can meet up anytime, but I don't hear back from her. Nothing changes at the transit company, and no article appears in the *Union-Bulletin* about the incident. For the vast majority of city residents who didn't hear about it, the incident didn't even happen.

The trans woman friend who let me know about the bus incident is going through her own crisis at home. Her wife, whom she married a decade before she transitioned, laments that she doesn't want to become a lesbian, and that this whole transsexual thing is bad for her business selling insurance. My trans friend's brother calls her regularly to remind her that she's going to hell. I meet up with her to see how she's doing and she runs her French-manicured fingers around the top of her coffee mug. She tried to take money out at the bank and discovered that her spouse had cleaned out the account. When she drove home, punching in the speed dial digits to call her wife and demanding to know what was going on, she found the house, including their daughter's room, cleared of belongings. I watch her hands shake as she talks to me, her words darting through the air to me, rapid-fire, like someone trying to get their words out before the sobs start rolling in. The court has offered her visitation, as if that is some kind of gift. In a state with common property laws, somehow the court system has found other responses to the breakup of her marriage and family. She looks at me and tells me she doesn't know what to do next. I have no good answers for her.

3. Health Care: I'm the executive director of an HIV nonprofit, which is the legacy of a group of Walla Wallans who saw in the mid-1980s that nothing was happening for people who had HIV and who realized the city needed an organization to help people. Twenty-eight years later, one of the hospitals in town has not gotten it together to remove their stigmas around the virus. They still insist that volunteers working in their facility be HIV-negative, despite the illegality of such a requirement, and more than once they have told my clients that they don't know how to work with HIV-positive people and that they should go to Seattle to get care.

I hear the front door to my office open, and I look up to see a man in his mid-fifties, reasonably healthy, with a paunch above his belt that is smaller than mine. He wants to get tested for HIV. He holds his hands together as he gives me the completed questionnaire we use to measure risk of exposure to the virus. I read it over and find nothing on it that should concern him. He doesn't claim to have had sex in more than a year, as far back as the questionnaire goes. He's not an injection drug user. I ask him if he's here for a specific reason or concerned about an exposure. His answer: His platelet count is high, and his doctor who knows he's gay suggested he may have HIV. There are many reasons why a platelet count could be high, like a simple infection or prescription side effect totally unrelated to anal sex and HIV. We talk a little about maybe going to see another physician, one who could administer their own HIV tests instead of sending him off to a nonprofit. I run a rapid test on him so that I can give him his negative result right away and hopefully some peace of mind, even though nothing in his background warrants the rapid test protocol.

In Walla Walla, we on the LGBTQ spectrum talk to each other in something like a stage whisper when we ask about physician and dentist recommendations. If a doctor lectures us about the health consequences of being gay, that experience travels around like a chain email, until the word is out that so-and-so considers proselytizing part of their Hippocratic Oath. Trans folk will talk about "that doctor who's willing to prescribe hormones" in a backdoor way like we just found a new heroin dealer willing to give us our fix. Conversations about doctors in the city include that time the doctor came in before my knee surgery and asked if he could pray with my partner and me, or when one of my clients moved to Spokane, three hours away, because he couldn't find a surgeon in Walla Walla who would operate on an HIV-positive person. There's the VA physician who told a veteran that he could work with him on his diabetes but not his HIV diagnosis, and the infectious diseases doctor who told a gay man to live a straight—meaning celibate—life so that he never exposed anyone else to HIV. Never mind that he had an undetectable viral load and had been educated on using condoms. With all of the national focus about health care reform, the question of what kind of health care LGBTQ people receive is almost never brought up.

LGBTQ health care reveals all that is weak in the US system of physicians, nurses, insurance companies, health technology, and regulation. Often medical coverage doesn't cover transgender people across a whole swath of procedures, like Pap smears for trans men or prostate exams for trans women, and many insurance plans, hardly ever written by trans people, have exclusions for vague procedures for things like "gender surgery." Here in Walla Walla, the Internet is the primary care source for several trans women, who do their own health research on everything from estrogen dosages to breast augmentation, and alternative methods of hair removal. Desperate people order hormones from other countries, or beseech friends for some of their prescriptions, even when there are huge penalties for such things. Testosterone is a Schedule III controlled substance, and giving it to a friend is a Class B felony, punishable by up to ten years in prison.

I drive 215 miles to Portland, Oregon, clicking through the radio stations until I find a song that I like. I'm on my way to see a doctor who will do good work without regard to my trans status, who understands some of my special medical needs as a trans man. This physician sees hundreds of trans patients, which I think is a bonus because to date there have been zero studies of transgender men and women, and next to no medical literature on how our needs may differ from cis people. If I break my arm in Walla Walla, I'm not going to drive three and a half hours to get care from her, but locating my primary care doctor four hours away is preferable to the physician who insisted on finding my prostate as part of my annual exam. I get a Pap smear every so often, but I've received six separate pieces of advice on how frequently I need to get them, so I go for a number somewhere in the middle and hope for the best.

4. Legal Protections: When I still lived in the nation's capital, I was a small part of a broad effort to pass an antidiscrimination amendment to the city's human rights law.[iii] The amendment was designed to cover "gender identity or expression," because until that point, gender nonconforming individuals only had "personal appearance" to use in a complaint, and it was clunky at best. We worked under the radar of both the mainstream and the gay press because we were concerned that any media attention would bring out opposition. What we didn't expect was that such opposition would be from two gay men who were spearheading marriage equality in the District of Columbia and who thought that our campaign would siphon political capital away from their efforts. When the city's Human Rights Office held a public hearing on the issue of the amendment, they attended and spoke against our campaign, and one of their points to justify their argument was the idea that this law would allow men to wear dresses and assault women in public restrooms.

I bring up this moment because it's an idea that gets trotted out nearly every time a municipality considers offering protections to trans and gender nonconforming people. In the 237-year history of the United States of America, this restroom calamity has never occurred. Not even once. Perhaps men who would assault women feel no need to change their clothes first. Perhaps trans women just want to urinate in peace. I become suspicious about why this idea of dress-wearing assaulters comes up repeatedly when we talk about equal access to public restrooms. But when we start talking about rural towns like Walla Walla, one of the effects of this mythology is to shut down calls for trans rights in public spaces before they even begin. In Walla Walla there are several "family restrooms" with a single toilet and a locking door, in places as varied as the YMCA, the community college, and older office buildings. These any-gender zones have escaped public comment, in part perhaps because not many people are aware that trans people live here—your family friendly policy is my quiet toilet. But refraining from a community discussion is not the same as progress.

A few years ago a trans woman seeking a bed at the sole

women's shelter was turned away, the supervisor suggesting she drive out to Portland instead, as if it were simple to afford the fifty dollars in gas, not to mention a car. This made her one of the 29 percent of transgender people turned away from temporary shelters.[iv] Another homeless trans woman kept her status quiet to all but a couple of friends and stayed in the men's shelter instead, where she was repeatedly harassed by other homeless people who read her as a gay man. She hitchhiked out of town after six months. Some lesbians who look too butch have problems getting hired here, and more than one gay man I've known in Walla Walla has been propositioned by married men who used their ability to hire and fire as a carrot-and-stick modulation of their offers. There is little confidence here that if one were to appeal to state antidiscrimination laws as protection that they wouldn't face retribution locally.

5. **Solidarity:** Walla Walla is small, fiercely independent, as it barely feels the pulse of Washington DC, or any city, from so far away. In a conservative environment like this LGBTQ people band together a little more closely, even when we're not the best of friends. Most folks here know each other, either because they grew up together or because there's little space for anonymity here. Our contact with each other gives us an opportunity to humanize what are often abstractions on the news or web. Maybe in a tighter space we can see more clearly the linkages between the disparate letters L G B T Q, and out of necessity, stand up for each other better.

A small town does offer a slower pace, a little relief from the frantic quality of denser communities. There's more time at the beginning and end of the day, fewer traffic bottlenecks, an easier walk to buy a coffee and read through greeting cards because a friend's birthday is coming up. If there's no gay bar in town, there is a breakfast restaurant where young lesbians can hold hands and not get harassed while they dig through a bowl of shrimp and grits as big as a soccer ball. There are more gay- and lesbian-owned businesses in town than ever, and area parties are sporadic connection sites for socializing across the local LGBTQ community. When speakers come to town, a sizable percentage of us are in attendance, bringing back the talking points to our friends who weren't there. If any of us encounters trouble, the news travels quickly like in an old game of Telephone. In Walla Walla we are more concerned with our common goals and responding to hardship than with our differences. Hardly anybody here talks about marriage equality like it was our top goal, even as two of my bowling teammates ask me to get ordained online so I can officiate their wedding next to the sprawling Pioneer Park in the middle of the city. And that is how Walla Walla County celebrated its first lesbian wedding, next to a small flock of chattering peacocks in the aviary.

And as soon as we finish, I get a text message on my phone, asking if I would please mentor a woman in town who is starting transition. *Of course,* I type back.

Notes

[i] Miller, Sean J, "The Gay Marriage Price Tag: $30 Million for Four States, and Not Even Brad Pitt Can Guarantee a Win," Takepart, October 31, 2012, http://www.takepart.com/article/2012/10/31/marriage-equality-campaign-price-tag-nears-30m-brad-pitt-donation.

[ii] Grant, Jaime M., Lisa A. Mottet, Justin Tanis, Jack Harrison, Jody L. Herman, and Mara Keisling, "A Report of the National Transgender Discrimination Survey," (Washington: National Center for Transgender Equality and National Gay and Lesbian Task Force, 2011), http://www.thetaskforce.org/reports_and_research/ntds.

[iii] http://dctranscoalition.wordpress.com/2006/05/28/transgender-people-in-dc-won-clear-protections-against-discrimination/.

[iv] Mottet, L., & Ohle, J, "Transitioning Our Shelters: A Guide to Making Homeless Shelters Safe for Transgender People," (New York: The National Coalition for the Homeless and the National Gay and Lesbian Task Force Policy Institute, 2003), http://www.thetaskforce.org/downloads/reports/reports/TransitioningOurShelters.pdf.

Sailor Holladay

Beyond Having

Growing up in a poor and violent family, I was stuck too many times in the middle of nowhere: in a school bus, on the side of the road waiting for a money order to arrive at general delivery. In a cabin, without electricity or running water, hungry for our welfare check and food stamps to come on the first. At a motel, unable to secure permanent housing, not knowing where we would go next. I was babysitter to my two younger brothers while our mom and dad fought, until I was called in as Mom and Dad's marriage counselor. Being poor means to wait, and being a poor kid with parents consumed by their relationship turmoil, means to wait to escape.

Marriage seemed to come two ways: broke and full of domestic violence, trauma bonding, and misery, like my parents' union; or of the middle-class television variety: *Growing Pains* and

Family Ties. Prime time representations of relationships felt as unattainable to me as the economic status and social capital TV characters had. By the time I saw Roseanne and Dan Conner's marriage—which was more stable, more blue-collar, and funnier than the one in my own home life, but still more familiar than the rest of television—I had already made up my mind that I wouldn't have kids and I wouldn't marry. I was nine. To choose to not marry was a political choice against all I saw marriage as standing for: violence, denial, and isolation.

While my queerness and trans identity later influenced my choice to not marry, only recently did I realize that, along with home ownership, I've been priced out of marriage. An online dating site popped up on my computer recently: "One in four people say bad credit is a deal breaker," the ad flashed. With over $100,000 in student loan debt, I am not in the most desirable fiancée category. The number of us heavily burdened with student debt is only rising, increasing the number of supposedly undesirable fiancées. Credit bureaus are now using who our Facebook friends are to determine our creditworthiness. This practice, if nothing else, shows how increasingly class segregated we are as a society, and how almost impossible it is for poor people to get out of poverty. Underneath large sums of debt that prevent us from marrying and owning homes, where can low-income, single people house our passions?

I've been in a romantic relationship with another low-income/ no-economic-assets person for seven years, and the fact that neither of us want to marry (or have kids, or practice a religion) influences our staying together. Both of us have felt pressure as thirtysomethings from other people we've dated to marry compulsorily—that marriage is just what you're supposed to do to deepen your love, that marriage is the logical next step. Along with polyamorous ethics informing our decision to not marry, working nonstop and paying off both our debts, so we can get into more debt for houses, cars, kids, and pets, would severely constrain the flexibility needed to pursue creative endeavors.

Despite the barriers, poor people are really good at building relationships. We know relationships are the most important resource there is. Queer punk communities have popularized mutual aid, at least as a concept, but poor people have always practiced it. An alternative to marriage in the queer community I'm a part of is communal housing and communal land ownership. A site of queer utopia. However, often times, a queer person with access to financial resources owns the house and other queers live in it with them, reproducing dynamics of familial disparity. Through cultural differences and lack of access to money, poor queers are priced out of these supposed queer utopias. There are so many skills poor folks have to contribute to communal projects that may not involve money. We have a lot to teach about the impermanence of having, the impermanence of relationships, the impermanence of home. We know what to do when shit hits the fan. Without the privilege or entitlement to "having it all," we've had to see beyond the set of currently available alternatives and develop strategies for thriving creatively in the current economic system.

Both my mom and the character of Roseanne have stated their regrets on marrying. Both presumably heterosexual women wanted something more for themselves and their children, but didn't know what that would be or where they could plug into society to get it. During their biggest fight, complete with object throwing and Roseanne's destruction of the television set she said Dan was addicted to, Dan accuses Roseanne of failing as a mother. Roseanne retorts, "The only way I failed as a mother is to let Becky and Darlene get married so young that they threw their whole life away on a man, just like I did." Before my mom married, she was an actress in a dinner theater, and in her most vulnerable moments has told me she regrets not pursuing those dreams. This culture propagates and then profits off of our feelings of not-enoughness, of feeling we have to marry in order to have social value or even self-worth.

I want a queer utopia, where I have a polyamorous marriage first with myself, then with my passions, and then with all of my relationships. For me, it's a privilege, a freedom to not marry. Marriage, queer or not, still looks like a road to social and economic isolation. Coming out as a queer teen, I defied the expectations that I be heterosexual, married, and childbearing. How can we apply that defiance so many of us asserted in our youth to the current economic system, with the goal of increasing intimacy and creativity in all of our relationships? There's so much merit in LGBTQ folks fighting for something we have been excluded from. But what's next? What exists beyond that having?

Judith Barrington

When Outlaws Marry

We were a couple for more than thirty-four years, and then we got married. A good friend who has a Universal Life Church certificate married us in Washington State, only a few miles up the highway from where we live in Oregon. We drove there because, as I write now, Washington has done the honorable thing and adopted marriage equality laws, while Oregon lags behind. It's only a matter of time, though. Even the most homophobic states will, in the end, surely allow same-sex marriages, and Oregon is not particularly homophobic. In fact by the time you read this, our state may have joined the expanding group of equal-marriage states; you may even be wondering what all the fuss was about.

Now that we are hitched, Ruth and I are finally entitled to all the federal benefits and responsibilities of marriage. For the many years we've been together and for all the time that preceded our meeting, even in childhood, I felt like an outlaw. And in many ways I *was* one.

I was proud of my outlaw status, especially in the seventies and eighties when my life was full of protest: social change activism, and various attempts, legal and illegal, to make life fairer, especially for women, lesbians, and gay men. Over time, that outsiderness became less exciting, perhaps because our methods of trying to change the world grew tamer, but I never gave up on working for justice one way or another. When marriage equality began to seem like a real possibility, I supported the efforts of thousands of dedicated activists and got involved, even though it wasn't a matter of great importance to me—at least not emotionally. I had no romantic notions about weddings. No desire to don a tux and choose music for a gathering in a vineyard or a fancy beach hotel. No need to replace vows made long ago and broken once in a while only to be remade in the context of a very long partnership.

So for a while we remained outlaws, still banned from the country club of marriage that, like certain clubs, excludes people because of their lifestyle choices, their race, or various aspects of their status. We had never much fancied joining that club, but now we felt obliged to batter down its doors, especially since so many good people were working to change the rules. The fact that they've finally allowed us to join is cause for celebration, indeed. But it doesn't mean we have to like the golf course, the dress code, or the people we meet in the bar. As one old feminist asked me recently, "Does this mean we're free to criticize marriage again?"

Having been together for so long, we had, of course, taken care of all the practical matters we could to compensate for being denied the automatic benefits of marriage. We had made wills, given each other the right to make decisions in medical emergencies, and so on. But now we sought advice and discovered that to be married would bring substantial financial advantages. To ignore the hard work of the LGBTQ community would be churlish; to ignore the good news coming to us next tax day would be downright foolish. So we did it with as little hoopla as possible. A quick signing of the papers in a Washington park, a toast or two, and a delicious salmon dinner on a summer evening with our obliging friend and her partner.

We have no intention of preserving the date of this marriage as an anniversary. We've already had thirty-four anniversaries on the date we named the beginning of our relationship (and outlaws with no wedding day do have to choose an appropriate one). Next year, on our chosen date in July, we will revisit Mount Adams, where we first camped in a high meadow with our dogs and discussed what we wanted to do with our lives. We're not sure we can hike that far up now, and damned sure we're not sleeping in a tent on the ground, but we'll certainly take the current dog and hope to see a sunset like that first one.

I'm not naive enough to think the fight for equality is over, and even as the law expands to include us, I know prejudice will remain, just as it has around racial issues; however, I do believe the scales are tilting in the direction of fairness. Many religions are opposed to us on spurious theological grounds, but one also hears a wide range of other silly objections: gay marriage will somehow mysteriously destroy straight marriages (spontaneous combustion upon seeing a married gay couple?); lesbians can't be trusted with children; the only purpose of marriage should be procreation—this in spite of the fact that plenty of older people, people unable to give birth, or people who just aren't into babies, get married with impunity. There is no explanation for any of these objections except bigotry, which is fear verging on panic and does not deal in logic. It is worn down slowly and, I hope in part, by seeing and knowing people like us.

| | |

When I look back over my lifetime, more than sixty years, I'm inclined to burst into the song our friend Kevin sings in his deep bass, smooth-as-treacle voice: "Who would've thunk it?" Indeed, it's astonishing how fast it all happened, and when I say that, I mean social change relating to gays, lesbians, bisexuals, and transgender people, though I might also be saying it about my own life. Can I really have been in a committed relationship with Ruth for half my life? Can it possibly be forty years since consciousness-raising, poster-defacing, internecine wars between radical and socialist feminists, to say nothing of the lesbian sex outlaws, who transgressed even ordinary transgression? Back then we never dreamed that the UK, where I fought many of my battles, and the United States, where I have lived for thirty-five years, would grant us marriage rights. It would never have occurred to us to put it on our agenda; after all, America had failed—and still has failed—to ratify equal rights for women. And why would we dream of altars and white dresses, when we were busy critiquing the institution of marriage? (We were fond of explaining the "rule of thumb" which came from an old law that forbade a man to beat his wife with a stick wider than his thumb.) All we wanted was to march in our patched jeans and yell about rape and abortion, incest and domestic violence. There were plenty of things to fight for before marriage, which in any case most of us despised.

Now that things are leveling out a little, my fears are different than they used to be. For a long time I feared being attacked in the street if I walked hand in hand with another woman (still possible but less on my mind); I feared that the antigay activists would burn down my house (they did shoot a bullet through the front window during one nasty antigay initiative campaign); I feared being shunned by straight people I liked. I feared being treated differently as a couple or treated not as a couple at all (as happened often when we were first together). There was a lot to worry about, but one of the worries that preoccupies me now is a new one: I'm afraid all that history, all that activism, all that passion, will be forgotten. I worry that younger people, who, in the West, live in a place far friendlier to LGBTQ folk than most parts of the world, have no idea how it felt to live in a society structured around homophobia, a world that targeted us legally, socially, and physically.

Even more than fearing the loss of our history, I fear future generations will never understand how being hated for who we were changed our personalities, destroyed our ambitions and our confidence, and sometimes drove us literally crazy, sending us to mental institutions that prescribed forgetfulness in the form of drugs or erased memories of a lover with electroshock "therapy." It's so much easier to track laws, marches, speak-outs, and occupations of events like Miss World than it is to track the internal erosion of energy, ambition, and compassion that damaged so many, or at least distracted us for so many years. We suffered from broken relationships, spent a fortune on therapy, and came to our real work, our relative sanity, or, like me, our ability to experience real joy, late in our lives.

| | |

For many of us it's a stretch to think of our own lives as history, yet I know I have lived through and around and in the middle of historic events that weave in and out of my personal story, that in a way have *become* my story. As writer Patricia Hampl says, if we neglect to tell this personal version of the past, someone else will do it for us. "That," she claims, "is the scary political fact."[i]

Because that prospect is indeed scary, I have tried to write memoirs of my life. I don't want a historian to write it for me. Nor do I want anyone growing up in this new climate of acceptance to remain ignorant of how thousands of us fought against what

Adrienne Rich called "the forces they had ranged against us and the forces we had ranged within us."ii Having witnessed extraordinary change—change that seems to come faster and faster like the rest of life in this technological age—I feel compelled by both passion and responsibility to share a few pieces of one life, in the hope that they illustrate something.

I am happy now living in a much more friendly community than ever before, but I also know how much time it took before I could trust it—time I try not to think of as wasted. I know how damaged I was by growing up believing I was a pervert. I can see why my relationships fell apart, given that I had no sense of being entitled to love and respect, nor did I feel able to give those things freely to another person, even one I wanted to love.

I don't believe that queers, even in an accepting climate, will suddenly become just like straight people. We have had different experiences growing up that left us with a more ironic and anti-authoritarian attitude than much of the mainstream. Perhaps that will not be true forever, but I am of a generation, some of whom still value dwelling outside the mainstream, or at least on the precarious edge, where how it used to be meets how it is now. When it is called for, being antiauthoritarian is useful; but to hang on to it as an outdated badge of honor is to be stuck in adolescence, even into middle and old age. The trick must be to move on into what has been won in the name of equality, but to hang on to our vigilance, to maintain our solidarity in the face of possible backlash, and to cede gracefully to a new situation that we old fighters hardly yet recognize.

There has been some healing among older lesbians, and there have also been tragic failures to heal. There have been women who spent their lives hiding and then realized they wanted to come out, but it was too late: they were too sick, too habituated to self-hatred, or just too tired to give it a try. We must remember them, just as we must remember the activists, among whom I count myself, whose stubborn determination has given everyone a chance for a better life—a life that includes, but goes far beyond, the choice to be married.

Notes

[i] Patricia Hampl, "Memory and Imagination," in *I Could Tell You Stories: Sojourns in the Land of Memory*, (W. W. Norton: New York, 1999), 32.

[ii] Adrienne Rich, "Twenty One Love Poems," in *The Dream of a Common Language*, (W. W. Norton: New York, 1978).

Mel Wells

Turbo

It took me sixteen years to admit to myself that I had a crush on my volleyball coach at Pocatello High School, in southeastern Idaho. Coach Billie was barely out of college, a paradox of athletics and engineering nerdiness, who described her own gait as "lumberjack" and wore her hair cropped, but also wore a dress to the big game against our cross-town rivals.

I was a blonde, Amazonian sophomore whose friends sometimes called "Turbo" because I approached everything—homework, crafts, cleaning—with a zealous impatience bordering on mania. I still do. But I'd forgotten about those late afternoons practicing in the gym, shoes squeaking, sweat dripping, a tight feeling in my lower belly whenever Coach Billie addressed me.

These memories were buried deep, but one of my few friends from high school posted an article on Facebook that dipped inside of me and stirred.

In the photo, I immediately recognized the painted boulder sitting on the front lawn of a brick building. There is an old tradition at Pocatello High School to paint "the rock" for important games, graduations, reunions, and so on. This time, it was painted white with the words, "We miss you...TURBO." I did a double take. There was also a picture of a blonde girl. I clicked the link.

The headline said that a female student had committed suicide, followed by a phrase I was unprepared for: "Family says teen was bullied for sexual orientation." My throat was too tight to gasp. I kept reading.

Maddie Stanger-Hollifield was a sophomore at "Poky." We climbed those same stairs, sat in those same classrooms, practiced volleyball and basketball in that same gym, changed in that same locker room, and navigated those same hallways, lined with huge framed collages of alumni dating back to the late 1800s. It's certain she passed the Class of 2000 photos many times, walking under my picture in the bottom row. Her nickname was "Turbo." She was out to her family about her sexuality, whereas I am only now adjusting to the fact that I've been attracted to women for as long as I've known what attraction feels like.

When I walked those scuffed halls in the late nineties, I passed under the graduation photos of my great-grandparents, grandparents and their siblings, and my parents' cousins. They were all Mormon. In high school, so was I.

Every weekday I crossed West Clark Street to attend Seminary. The building was squat and ugly compared to Poky's soaring Art Deco masonry and roofline turreted with stone urns. I attended four years of religion classes, memorizing verses from The Book of Mormon and vacillating between yearnings for rebellion and acceptance.

Maddie and I probably gave the same amount of thought to getting married: almost none. She, too, probably wasn't thinking about health insurance benefits and filing joint taxes and adoption costs. I hope she experienced that nervous flutter when seeing her crush. But I cannot picture either of us walking around our hometown holding hands with another female without fearing for our safety.

Pocatello is not an easy place to be different. It's the kind of place where "member" refers to being a baptized Mormon, and every other lifestyle is lumped into "nonmember." It's a place where California Mormons move to buy cheap McMansions and have plenty of members for their kids to date. It's a place where "the church" means Mormon—where the freshly engaged couples in the community section of the newspaper are in their early twenties and registered at Walmart. Coffee shops are vastly outnumbered by chapels. The only bookstore is Deseret Book, owned by the church.

There used to be a Waldenbooks in the mall. My paternal grandfather, a professor at Idaho State University, and I would spend hours there browsing the shelves and reading in the aisles until Grandma Wells joked about dragging us out by our hair. But I knew they were proud of my bookish, insatiable curiosity.

My maternal grandfather worked for Union Pacific and taught me more hands-on skills: how to drive his truck while pulling the boat trailer, how to back the boat down into American Falls Reservoir, and how to drive the boat while pulling a water-skier. Long before I knew the word "feminism," I knew what it felt like to be treated as equal to my male cousins.

The only times I felt limitations on my gender were in my religion, with its stern emphasis on heterosexual roles. When I heard that the Apostle Boyd K. Packer listed the three enemies of the church as "feminists, intellectuals, and homosexuals," his words stung. All three were in me, and I fought to suppress them. Even in my journals, I never admitted to crushing on my coach, instead writing that her eyes were like chocolate.

It's hard to explain just how much courage it must have taken for Maddie to come out as gay in our hometown. The area is

50 percent Mormon and more conservative than Utah. In high school, my best friend referred to herself as a nonmember and, despite never drinking or smoking, made jokes about her Mormon friends' parents being afraid that she was corrupting their children. I knew she was laughing to hide the hurt.

I imagine the types of guys who asked Maddie out were those same Mormon boys I knew: teenagers who've been told their Priesthood authority comes from God, and that they were born to lead. When I imagine their reactions to her honesty about liking girls, it makes me queasy.

Even as a member, every time I skipped Seminary or swore in practice, the other Mormons would glance at each other, tight-lipped, and I was pushed to the social fringes. Most of my teenage journal entries are scribbled laments about feeling like an outcast. I rarely dated, and my best friend and I joked about people thinking we were lesbians. She was not the only kidder hiding painful truths.

I left Pocatello two days after graduation, but it took me another seven years to come out as a nonbeliever to my family, after I'd built a stable life in Portland, Oregon, where I gravitated to the queer community, noting how similar our coming-out stories were. Now I find myself facing another closet door, hesitantly pushing. After seeing the news about Maddie, I texted my mother: "I heard a girl at Poky committed suicide because she was being bullied about being gay. What the heck? That's heartbreaking." She never responded.

At least she still talks to me. My father does not. But gradually, cautiously, most of my family members have learned that I'm still the same person. It's taken me a while to trust that love—to believe they aren't trying to pull me back into the faith. I'm scared to upset the fragile balance we've struck.

I confess to wondering, why bother? I'm out at my work and in my community. What is the value of visibility if I lose communication? I cringe imagining my sweet grandmother, my cousins (who are like siblings), and god forbid, my mother, picturing me in some sex scene à la the film *Blue is the Warmest Color*. I keep putting off having them visit the church-owned website, MormonsAndGays.com, to read the pandering language about how their "lives are impacted" and they are "working through difficult challenges" as though they're "dealing with" someone who is binge drinking on the regular and buying kiddie porn, instead of falling in love.

According to this website, same-sex *attraction* is okay, but *acting* on it is a sin. I currently live 961 miles away from my girlfriend, so technically I'm not "acting on" my attraction very frequently. But what about my giddy grin when she texts or calls me, or how I think she's beautiful in her photos, or the way I feel lit up inside when she smiles on Skype, or how I want her to feel the same? What is "acting on," anyway?

My feelings for her are more than tingles when she touches me, or light-headedness when we kiss. I've known lust. When she and I are together, fully clothed, arms around each other, just talking and laughing, I find myself thinking, *This feels like home*.

And while Pocatello will always be my hometown, I am no prodigal daughter contemplating a return. Sometimes I meet other ex-Mormons, often gay ones, and I feel the recognition of fellow refugees, speaking in our mother tongue and swapping stories about adapting to new cultures. We escaped! It got better!

I will never get to have this conversation with Maddie. Although we never met, I'm sure our acquaintances, even our bloodlines, have several tendrils linking us together. Who knows how many times, during my visits to those high-desert plains, we drove or even walked past each other, oblivious allies. But this little member of my tribe did not make it. This crushes me.

When I do tell my family I'm dating a female, I don't want them wondering who is the "man" and who is the "woman" in our relationship. I want them to remember the delicious sensation of falling in love—of staying up talking till 2:00 a.m. and laughing at each other's jokes, thinking, *Oh, thank god, they get me!* I want them to remember the exhilarating sensation of being known and appreciated. Because being gay is not all about sex. It is not even all about marriage. Being gay is about love.

I hope my family will recognize that my love for them and my gratitude for everything they have taught me—who they helped me become—has nothing to do with my sexuality. I dream of them reacting with as much love and acceptance as Maddie's family gave her. And I hope that by realizing someone they love is gay, my family will see the humanity behind the labels.

I also confess, I looked up Coach Billie while online and discovered she recently came out in a Pocatello city council meeting, testifying in support of a nondiscrimination ordinance. Her bravery made me tremble, especially when I read some of the comments. But I also feel a small budding of hope. I can't help but dream of change—of the day a sophomore volleyball player at PHS develops a crush on her female coach, confesses it to teammates in squeals and giggles, and is teased in the same affectionate, silly way that a crush on a dreamy male English teacher would merit. I dream of a gentler handling of each other's hearts.

And while I cannot legislate my family's hearts, perhaps I can be a little turbo again, in the sense of pushing forward to this future of more honesty and more love—toward an understanding that gay love does not threaten straight love. Love cannot threaten love. After all, according to the one Bible verse that still resonates within me, even God is love. Perhaps I should have more faith in it.

Contributor Biographies

Ben Anderson-Nathe is an associate professor and program director of Child and Family Studies at Portland State University. He holds graduate degrees in social work, public policy, and community education with a focus in youth studies. He has a passion for working with youth and supporting adults to engage differently with young people. His teaching and scholarship center on justice and equity, sexuality and gender, and the lives of young people. Ben currently lives in Portland, Oregon, with Michael, Sophie, and Margaret.

Ryka Aoki has as an MFA in creative writing from Cornell University, and is a writer, performer, and a professor of English at Santa Monica College. She was a charter member of the Transgender Advisory Committee for Asian Pacific Islanders for Human Rights. Aoki appears in the trans documentaries *Diagnosing Difference* and *Riot Acts* as well as the anthologies *Gender Outlaws: The Next Generation* and *Transfeminist Perspectives*. Aoki's chapbook, *Sometimes Too Hot the Eye of Heaven Shines*, won the RADAR's 2010 Eli Coppola Chapbook Contest. Aoki, a former national judo champion and the founder of the International Transgender Martial Arts Alliance, is head instructor of Supernova Martial Arts. She currently resides in Los Angeles, California.

Judith Barrington was born in Brighton, England, and has lived in Oregon since 1976. She received the 2001 Lambda Book Award for *Lifesaving: A Memoir*, which was also a PEN/Martha Albrand Award for the Art of the Memoir finalist and recently appeared in German translation. Her book *Writing the Memoir: From Truth to Art* is a best seller. She is also the author of three poetry collections, and her fourth will be published in the spring of 2015. She has served on the faculty of the University of Alaska's low-residency MFA program and teaches workshops throughout the United States, Britain, and Spain. She lives with her partner in Portland, Oregon.

Trish Bendix is a writer and editor in Los Angeles, California. She has written about the intersection of queer women and pop culture and media as the managing editor of AfterEllen.com since 2008. Trish's work has been published in *Cosmopolitan, Slate, The Village Voice, Time Out Chicago, Out, Punk Planet, Bitch, The Frisky, AlterNet,* and *The Huffington Post.* Her fiction has appeared in *The Q Review, Provacateur,* and CellStories, and she has an essay in the 2010 Seal Press anthology, *Dear John, I Love Jane.*

Jeanne Cordova is a co-founder of the West Coast LGBTQ movement, and the recipient of a Lambda Literary Award, a Publishing Triangle Award, a Golden Crown Literary Award, a Stonewall Book Award, and was included in the 2013 Rainbow List: The GLBT Roundtable of the American Library Association for her recent memoir, *When We Were Outlaws.* As a longtime community organizer, she chaired the Butch Voices LA Conference in 2010 and the West Coast Lesbian Conference in 1973. As president of the Stonewall Democratic Club, she was an openly gay Kennedy delegate to the 1980 Democrat National Convention. She lives with her partner of twenty-five years in Hollywood Hills, California.

Joseph Nicholas DeFilippis was born and raised in New York City. He graduated from Vassar College and earned a master's in social work from Hunter College School of Social Work. He was the founding executive director of Queers for Economic Justice, an organization working with low-income and homeless LGBT people. He has also worked with the Welfare Reform Network and the NYS LGBT Health and Human Services Network, and served as the director of SAGE/Queens, working with LGBT senior citizens. He was one of the main authors of the infamous 2006 BEYOND SAME-SEX MARRIAGE document. He currently teaches courses on family law and policy and sexuality at Portland State University while pursuing his doctorate. He lives in Portland, Oregon.

Tucker Garcia works as a groundskeeper and teaches poetry workshops at his local LGBTQ center in Springfield, Massachusetts.

Ariel Gore received a bachelor's degree from Mills College and a master's of journalism from UC Berkeley. She is the founder of *Hip Mama Magazine* and the author of many books, from nonfiction parenting guides like *The Hip Mama's Survival Guide* and *The Mother Trip*, her memoirs, *Atlas of the Human Heart* and *The End of Eve*, to her novel, *The Traveling Death and Resurrection Show*. Her essays, short stories, and poems have appeared in anthologies and publications from *Listen Up: Voices from the Next Feminist Generation* to *Salon*. Born on the Monterey Peninsula and raised in the Bay Area, Gore currently resides in Oakland, California, with her partner and son.

Penny Guisinger is a graduate of the Stonecoast MFA program at the University of Southern Maine. Her work has appeared in *Fourth Genre*, *River Teeth*, and *Solstice Literary Magazine*. Her essay "Coming Out" was a finalist in the 2013 *Fourth Genre* essay contest. Another essay, "Provincetown," was awarded an editor's choice award from *Solstice*. Her reviews appear in *The Quoddy Tides*. She is the founding organizer of Iota: The Conference of Short Prose. She lives with her (now legally recognized) wife in Trescott, Maine, where they spend their time gardening, walking the tidal line, and stacking firewood. She is raising her young children to be political activists.

Pamela Helberg is working on her memoir, an intimate look at what happens when the Perfect Lesbian Family falls apart, a story by turns humorous and heartbreaking. Her essay "Body Language" appeared in *Beyond Belief: The Secret Lives of Women in Extreme Religion*. She received an MA in creative writing from Western Washington University many years ago and is currently working on a master's degree in mental health counseling at Antioch University in Seattle. She enjoys running, kayaking, writing haikus, and hanging out with her writing buddies. She also blogs semi-regularly at pamelahelberg.com. She and her wife, Nancy, live in Bellingham, Washington.

Sailor Holladay is a writer, editor, teacher, film critic, and textile artist living in Portland, Oregon. Sailor was a Lambda Fellow in 2012 and holds an MFA in creative nonfiction from Mills College. Sailor's writing and art have appeared in the 2010 and 2014 National Queer Arts Festival visual art exhibitions, *Passage and Place*, *580 Split*, *Persistence: All Ways Butch and Femme*, *Gay Genius* comics anthology, *The Encyclopedia Project Vol. F-K*, Colony Collapse Disorder Radio, Enough.org, and *Without a Net: The Female Experience of Growing Up Working Class*.

Everett Maroon was raised in Hightstown, New Jersey. He received a BA in English from Syracuse University. He has released a memoir, *Bumbling into Body Hair*, and a YA novel, *The Unintentional Time Traveler* from Booktrope Editions. His work has been published in *Bitch Magazine*, GayYA.org, *RH RealityCheck*, and *Remedy Quarterly*, and he blogs at transplantportation.com. Maroon lives with his partner and two children in Walla Walla, Washington, and works actively to support and assist trans youth in his community.

A.M. O'Malley lived in thirteen towns in seven states in her first seventeen years. When asked where she's from, it's often easiest to simply say "America." Ms. O'Malley now lives in Portland, Oregon, and is the program director of a small arts non-profit. She teaches creative writing and collage arts at Portland Community College, and is a resident artist in the Literary Arts Writers in the Schools program. Ms. O'Malley won a 2014 Skidmore Prize for piloting and teaching in a creative writing program at the Columbia River Correctional Institution. Her work has appeared in various zines, lit magazines, and bathroom stalls. She recently finished a book of micro-essays called *What to Expect When You're Expecting Something Else*.

Minh Pham writes candidly about what it is to be gay or transgender in

Vietnam, where he was born. He received an MFA from UC Riverside. His nonfiction work has been published in *The Rattling Wall*, and his poetry in *Kartika Review* and *Mascara Literary Review*.

Casey Plett is the author of the short story collection *A Safe Girl To Love*, released in 2014 by Topside Press. She also wrote a column on transitioning for *McSweeney's Internet Tendency*, and her work has been featured in *Plenitude, Two Serious Ladies, Anomalous Press*, and other publications. She is from the Canadian Prairies and the Pacific Northwest and lives in Winnipeg, Manitoba.

Chelsia A. Rice is a cancer survivor and essayist living with her partner and two wiener dogs in Helena, Montana. As a daughter of a lesbian couple, she's been a life-long vocal advocate for equal rights. After receiving her MFA from the University of Idaho in 2008, she published "Tough Enough to Float" in the *Los Angeles Review*. Though it was the first essay she published, it was selected as a Notable Best American Essay for 2014. More of her writing can be found at About.com, PeripheralSurveys.com, and at Chelsiarice.com.

Charles Rice-González is a writer, community and LGBT activist, cofounder and executive director of BAAD! The Bronx Academy of Arts and Dance, and a distinguished lecturer in the English Department at Hostos Community College/CUNY. He received a BA in communications from Adelphi University and an MFA in creative writing from Goddard College. His debut novel, *Chulito*, received awards and recognitions from the ALA and the National Book Critics Circle. He co-edited *From Macho to Mariposa: New Gay Latino Fiction* with Charlie Vazquez, is an award-winning playwright, and serves on boards for the Bronx Council on the Arts and the National Association of Latino Art and Cultures. Rice-González received a 2014 Dr. Betty Berzon Emerging Writer Award.

Fabian Romero was born in Michoacán, Mexico, and came to the United States at the age of seven. As soon as they learned to write they began filling notebooks with bilingual poetry. They co-founded and participated in several writing and performance groups, including

Hijas de Su Madre, Las Mamalogues, and Mixed Messages: Stories by People of Color. Their poetry appears in *Troubling the Line: Trans and Genderqueer Poetry and Poetics* and in the upcoming Australian book *To the Exclusion of All Others: Queers Questioning Gay Marriage*. In 2014, they completed a BA with an emphasis on Writing and Education. They currently live in Olympia, Washington.

Francesca T. Royster was raised in Nashville, Tennessee, and Chicago, Illinois. She is a professor of English at DePaul University, and currently lives in Chicago, Illinois, with her partner and daughter. She is the author of two books: *Becoming Cleopatra: the Shifting Image of an Icon* and *Sounding Like a No-No: Queer Sounds and Eccentric Acts in the Post-Soul Era*.

B R Sanders studied psychology, law and society, and religion at Oberlin College, and earned a Ph.D. in the personality and social contexts area of the University of Michigan– Ann Arbor's Psychology Department. Outside of writing, B has worked as a research psychologist, a labor organizer, and a K-12 public education data specialist. They have published numerous short stories and one novel, *Resistance*, a story about radical lesbian elves. They blog at brsanderswrites.com. B lives in Denver, Colorado, with their family and two cats.

Regina Sewell received a Ph.D. in sociology from the Ohio State University and an M.Ed. in community counseling from the University of Dayton. She works as a psychotherapist, college professor, and singer-songwriter. Regina has a bi-monthly column, "InsightOut," in *Outlook Magazine*, and her essay "Sliding Away" was included in *Knowing Pains: Women on Love, Sex and Work in Our 40s*. Her book *We're Here! We're Queer! Get Used to Us!* was released in 2004. Regina lives with her wife and two cats in the Hudson Valley region of New York.

Jackson Shultz grew up in Waitsburg, Washington. He received his bachelor's degree in women's studies from Washington State University, and his master's degree in creative writing from Dartmouth College. His first book, *Transgender Portraits: An Oral History*, will be released in the fall of 2015 from the University Press of New England. Jackson works as a web programmer for the Geisel School of Medicine at Dartmouth, and teaches composition as an adjunct professor at New England College. Additionally, Jackson is the Outreach Coordinator for the Trans* Education, Activism, Community and Health (TEACH) Alliance, a non-profit dedicated to the well being of transgender individuals.

Kristopher Shultz hails from College Place, Washington. He attended Washington State University, where he received his bachelor's degree in women's studies. Kristopher is serving as the Family Shelter Case Manager at the Upper Valley Haven, a local homeless shelter, and working on his master's thesis on issues of queer youth homelessness. He intends to graduate from Dartmouth College with a master's in cultural studies in 2015. Kristopher also serves as the Education Director for the TEACH Alliance. To learn more about Kristopher's non-profit work, visit: www.teachalliance.com.

Meg Stone is the executive director of IMPACT Boston, an abuse prevention and self-defense training organization. She is a contributor to Cognoscenti, the opinion blog of the Boston NPR station. Her writing has been published in make/shift, *The Patriot Ledger* and the *Ms.* and *Bitch* blogs, as well as the anthologies *I Do/I Don't: Queers on Marriage* and *Pinned Down By Pronouns*. Whether Meg's love for musicals and extensive knowledge of show tune lyrics makes her more or less queer is a matter of opinion. She lives in the Boston area with her partner, Mal, who gets a little sick of the aforementioned show tunes but is usually a good sport.

Mel Wells was born and raised in Pocatello, Idaho. She earned a BA at Brigham Young University and an MS in book publishing at Portland State University. Her work has been published in *Pathos Literary Magazine, Salamander Magazine, Boneshaker: A Bicycling Almanac,* and *Spent: Exposing Our Complicated Relationship with Shopping.* She currently lives in Portland, Oregon, and spends her time surfing, biking, and working as the program coordinator for Literary Arts. Wells is also finishing a memoir about her experiences as a Mormon missionary in Belgium, titled *My Underwear Will Save Me.*

Emanuel Xavier grew up in New York's Bushwick area of Brooklyn. After enduring privation, abuse, and addiction, he transitioned into a force in the spoken word movement. He is the author of the novel *Christ Like* and several volumes of poetry, including *Nefarious* and *Pier Queen*. He was named an LGBT icon by the Equality Forum and received a Marsha A. Gomez Cultural Heritage Award, an NYC Council Citation, a World Pride Award, and was a finalist for Lambda Literary Awards and an International Latino Books Award. He edited *Mariposas: A Modern Anthology of Queer Latino Poetry* and *Me No Habla With Acento: Contemporary Latino Poetry*.

About the Editor

Carter Sickels is the author of the novel *The Evening Hour*. He is the recipient of the 2013 Lambda Literary Emerging Writer Award, a project grant from RACC, and an NEA Fellowship to the Hambidge Center for the Arts. His short stories and literary essays have appeared in a broad range of periodicals and anthologies, from *Appalachian Heritage* to *The Collection: Short Fiction from the Transgender Vanguard*. He lives in Portland, Oregon.

Index

Ooligan Press

Ooligan Press is a general trade publisher rooted in the rich literary tradition of the Pacific Northwest. Ooligan strives to discover works that reflect the diverse values and rich cultures that inspire so many to call the region their home. Founded in 2001, the press is a vibrant and integral part of Portland's publishing community, operating within the Department of English at Portland State University. Ooligan Press is staffed by graduate students working under the guidance of a core faculty of publishing professionals.

Project Managers

Meagan Lobnitz   Kate Marshall

Acquisitions

Brian Tibbets (manager)   Kate Marshall
Laurel Boruck

Editing

Sarah Currin-Moles (manager)   Kathryn Osterndorff
Katey Trnka (manager)   Sabrina Parys
Melissa Gifford   Mary Presnell
Alexandra Haehnert   Kurt Spickerman
Meagan Lobnitz   Geoff Wallace
Tenaya Mulvihill

Design

Riley Kennysmith (manager)   Brandon Sanford
Erika Schnatz (manager)   Margaret Schimming
Stephanie Podmore

Marketing & Promotions

Adam Salazar (manager)
Ariana Vives (manager)
Dory Athey
Michael Berliner
Melissa Gifford
Roberta Kelley
K Marthaler
Tina Morgan
Tenaya Mulvihill
Brian Parker
Sabrina Parys

Mary Presnell
Katy Roberts
Brandon Sanford
Margaret Schimming
Kurt Spickerman
Brian Tibbetts
Alison Townsend
Theresa Tyree
Camille Watts
Hayley Wilson

Digital

Meaghan Corwin (manager)

Melissa Gifford

Grant Writing

Alexa Goff
Lauren Lamson
Brian Tibbetts

Colophon

Untangling the Knot is set in Minion Pro, an Adobe Originals typeface designed by Robert Slimbach. It was inspired by classical, old style typefaces of the late Renaissance, a period of elegant, beautiful, and highly readable type designs.

Titles, including the front cover, are set in various weights of Univers. As a student in Zurich, Adrian Frutiger began work on Univers, which would eventually be released in 1957 by the Deberny & Peignot foundry in Paris. The design is a neo-grotesque, similar to its contemporary, Helvetica.